D1575545

FEB   2016

THE CAROLS OF CHRISTMAS

THE CAROLS OF CHRISTMAS

A Celebration of the Surprising Stories
Behind Your Favorite Holiday Songs

Andrew Gant

NELSON
BOOKS

An Imprint of Thomas Nelson

©2015 by Andrew Gant

Music Arrangements copyright © Andrew Gant, 2014

All rights reserved. No portion of this book may be reproduced, stored in a retrieval system, or transmitted in any form or by any means—electronic, mechanical, photocopy, recording, scanning, or other—except for brief quotations in critical reviews or articles, without the prior written permission of the publisher.

Published in Nashville, Tennessee, by Nelson Books, an imprint of Thomas Nelson. Nelson Books and Thomas Nelson are registered trademarks of HarperCollins Christian Publishing, Inc.

Thomas Nelson titles may be purchased in bulk for educational, business, fund-raising, or sales promotional use. For information, please e-mail SpecialMarkets@ThomasNelson.com.

"I Wonder As I Wander" by John Jacob Niles. Copyright © 1934 (Renewed) by G. Schirmer, Inc. (ASCAP). International Copyright Secured. All Rights Reserved. This Arrangement © Copyright 2015 G. Schirmer. Used by Permission of Chester Music Limited trading as G. Schirmer.

A version of this text was published in 2014 by Profile Books Ltd under the title *Christmas Carols*.

Library of Congress Control Number: 2015944228

ISBN: 978-0-7180-3152-7

Printed in the United States of America

15 16 17 18 19 RRD 6 5 4 3 2 1

For Kathy

Contents

CONTENTS

Introduction

nglish Christmas carols are a hodgepodge of nationalities and influences, like Americans themselves. Perhaps that's why they are so popular. They have the power to summon up a special kind of midwinter mood, like the aroma of mince pies and mulled wine and the twinkle of lights on a tree. It's a kind of magic.

How did they get that magic? Most of these songs were not composed as Christmas carols. Many were not "composed" at all. Almost all did not begin life with the words they have now. Some didn't have words at all. Several evolved from folk songs; some are evolving still. One much-loved carol started out as a song about a delinquent farmboy and a couple of dead cows. Many of the most "English" carols have at least one ancestor in another country, in the mountains of Austria or nineteenth-century America or a Pyrenean hillside; in Lutheran psalters, handsome volumes of illuminated plainsong or sturdy hymnbooks from Finland, first opened by the flickering light of a fire in some stone hall one dark evening, deep in the sixteenth century.

The origins of the word *carol* are almost as murky as the history of some of the tunes themselves. Most European languages, living and dead, have been quoted as the source of the word, though most writers agree that there is a dash of French in there somewhere.

In the beginning, a carol was a celebratory song, with dancing. There is no exclusive connection to Christmas. Music is in the traditional "stanza and burden" (or "verse and refrain") format. It certainly has nothing to do with church. In about 1400, the gory tale of *Sir Gawain and the Green Knight*, as translated by J. R. R. Tolkien, tells us: "The king lay at Camelot at Christmas-tide with many a lovely lord . . . to the court they came at carols to play . . . they danced and danced on, and dearly they carolled."[1] [1]

Choirs sang church music. Everyone else sang carols. Tolkien's version of *Sir Gawain* draws the distinction between "songs of delight, such as canticles of Christmas" and "carol-dances."

Folk carols on Christian themes were sung in the field and the graveyard, and on semi-magical processions round the parish. Their texts often cover the entire Christian worldview, from creation to resurrection. Today, we tend to just snip out the bits we want at Christmas, for example, "Tomorrow shall be my dancing day" and "The cherry-tree carol," which was not how our medieval forebears used these songs at all.

Fifteenth-century English carols began to take on some of the sophistication of the church composer. The texts are "macaronic," freely dropping Latin words and phrases into an English lyric:

There is no rose of such vertu
As is the rose that bare Jesu.
Res Miranda.

The music is in the ubiquitous verse-and-refrain format.

By the sixteenth century, the word *carol* could find itself loosely applied to any song with a seasonal connection, still definitely not just Christmas. An ancient and mysterious folk song appeared under the title "Corpus Christi Carol" in 1504. Court composer William Cornysh was paid the handsome sum of £20 for "setting of a Carrall upon Xmas day" at around the same time as Wynkyn de Worde included the entirely secular "Carol of hunting" in the collection that he (rather confusingly) called "Christmasse carolles" in 1521. One of William Byrd's consort songs from around the 1580s, designed to be sung at home, has the subtitle "A Caroll for New-Yeares Day." A text sung in church at Christmas could also be a carol, whether the words make any reference to the nativity or not. A 1630 publication refers to "Certain of David's Psalmes intended for Christmas Carolls fitted to the most common but solempne Tunes."[2] These "Carolls" are just the psalms of the day. Neither words nor music have any seasonal content.

Protestants wanted to grab the best tunes back from the devil and the pub. During the Reformation, secular songs and well-known chorales started to be used in worship. Compilers of tunes for psalm singing, hugely influential and popular, put them in their psalters. Alongside this went a passion for education. School songbooks sprang up everywhere. One such book, *Piae Cantiones ecclesiasticae velerum episcoporum*, is the source of a large number of our best-known carols. In France, dancing-masters and *chefs du choeur* started noting down little rustic *Noëls* and incorporating them into published collections, for teaching, playing, dancing, and singing, and sometimes adding new words. All feed into the tradition we have today.

In the mid-seventeenth century a more extreme brand of Protestantism took hold in England, with its stern disapproval of any kind of levity in church, or indeed anywhere else. The Puritans, famously, banned Christmas. As always, though, we need to see this in context. Puritans banned a lot of things. Christmas was not the mad, musical midwinter party we have come to know since. It went as part of a general assault on saints' days and elaborate ritual in church practice as a whole, and as part of a rather arcane dispute about which took precedence when a liturgical fast fell on the same day as Christmas. The jollity, of course, came back in a great whirl of enthusiasm at the Restoration in 1660. Carols, like life, were mainly an excuse for having fun. Songs about drinking, wassailing, drinking, eating, dancing, and drinking were especially popular.

The more measured Protestantism of the very last Stuarts— William, Mary, and Anne—made its own distinctive contribution. The beginnings of congregational hymn singing in the eighteenth century give us familiar carols like "While Shepherds Watched," still closely based on the old style of metrical psalm singing. These words have been sung to all sorts of different tunes, each one reflecting the social and religious preoccupations of the singers.

The Wesleys and Watts gave their followers lengthy devotions to sing on the dusty road, which have been absorbed into the popular consciousness. Watts's lovely "Cradle Song" turns up, suitably distorted by the Chinese whispers of an oral tradition, as the words of an English folk song. Parish churches, with their distinctive bands of instrumentalists and "West Gallery" choirs, mixed fashionable metropolitan musical style with a love of hymn singing and their own intensely local traditions to create something sturdy, uniquely English, and full of character.

In the mid-nineteenth century, antiquarians and folklorists like William Chappell began to collect and publish their native folk songs. There are several important books devoted just to Christmas carols. Joshua Sylvester (a pseudonym) illustrates this new spirit of historical enquiry, and acknowledges some of its pioneers, in the introduction to his own 1864 book:

> Forty years ago an antiquary wrote complainingly: "Carols begin to be spoken of as not belonging to this century, and yet no one, as I am aware of, has attempted a collection of these fugitives." Several gleaners since then, however, have entered the field. Mr. Davies Gilbert, Mr. Sandys, Dr. Rimbault, and Mr. Thomas Wright have each garnered their gleanings into little volumes. From these I have derived much assistance in the compilation of the present work.[3]

Sandys has turned out to be the most fruitful for our modern carol tradition, though, as Sylvester acknowledges, these early books overlap a good deal.

These men were compilers, working from existing sources like ballad sheets or the libraries of earlier collectors. The next stage, in the early twentieth century, was for the new generation of "gleaners" to go out into the highways and byways and hear folk carols for themselves. Cecil Sharp explains how it's done:

> Only a few weeks ago I asked two old men who were singing to me whether they knew a certain carol. One of them said that he did; the other, the elder of the two, shook his head doubtfully. Whereupon the younger singer stood up and, dragging his

companion up beside him, said encouragingly: "Stand up, and think you've got snow in your boots, and it'll come to you all right." And it did![4]

Most of the early books and ballad sheets didn't contain tunes. The oral tradition was so well established, you could happily assume your reader would already know them. Often it was enough simply to print the name of the tune, or, if the words were in a common meter, allow the singer to use any matching tune that he already knew. This

"... discordant caterwauling ...": carol-singing in London. The ubiquitous ballad broadside sheets have words and pictures, but no tunes.

contributed to the huge variety and lack of standardization about which tune goes with a particular text. Even when the same tune was used in different towns and villages, it could differ between one and the other. The same tune could exist in scores of versions, alike in essentials, quite different in detail. When Sharp and others started writing down the tunes as people actually sang them, it became clear how an oral tradition militates against uniformity. Stainer's "God Rest You Merry Gentlemen" has a different first note from Sharp's (the first degree of the scale instead of the fifth). Stainer got the tune from the streets of London. Sharp collected it in Cambridge. That interval of fifty miles shows up as the musical interval of a perfect fifth.

Some folk songs may well also involve the presence of a real author or composer. Sharp wrote:

> In several parts of England I have found carols which are peculiar to certain villages, by the inhabitants of which they are regarded as private possessions of great value, to be jealously guarded and retained for their own use. These are not traditional or folk-carols but the elementary compositions of simple musicians, very possibly of those who in the old days were members of the Church bands. They are easily distinguished from the popular carol by the formal nature of the music and words, and also by the fact that many of them are written in parts. Some of these compositions are by no means without merit. The melodies, if not inspired, are usually strong and sincere, and, plainly, the expression of genuine feeling.[5]

He quotes one, which, "while it lacks the freshness, the *naiveté*, and indeed pretty nearly all the typical and characteristic qualities of the folk carol, is nevertheless quite as good as some, and far better than many of the modern Christmas hymns annually sung in fashionable Churches and Chapels," adding, "there is, perhaps, no branch of folk-music in the creation of which the unconscious art of the peasant is seen to greater advantage than the carol."[6]

His tone appears slightly condescending to modern ears, but Sharp, king of the collectors, was unquestionably "strong and sincere," and a scholar.

Carol singing in the country: much more genteel.

The dedicated idealism of Sharp, Lucy Broadwood, J. A. Fuller Maitland, and others is of crucial importance in the story of the carol (although even then the word *carol* had not taken on its exclusively Christmassy connotation. A 1903 book specifically refers to "Easter carols and Christmas songs," and an important publication of 1924 collects what it calls *Fifty-two Songs for Christmas, Easter, and Other Seasons* under the catch-all title *The Cambridge Carol-Book*).

Many carols are clearly local variations or expansions on authored originals. Some have an artfulness that, as Sharp suggests, implies the existence of an author but with no clue as to who might have done the deed. Translations complicate things further, not just between languages, but from one style of religious practice or one century to another. Many fall between the cracks or slip down the back of the pew. So, if you occasionally get to the end of a chapter in this book slightly unsure about who wrote words or tunes or bits of either, me too. It's all part of the tradition.

Collecting songs in the field also, of course, exposes you to the vagaries of the various performers you happen to meet. Writing in the 1920s, Marjorie Kennedy-Fraser refers to the work of the Rev. Patrick Macdonald of Kilmore, Argyll, who published a book of two hundred airs in 1784:

> Apropos of the luck of the collector in hearing the best versions of airs, Macdonald remarks that in noting the tunes, "perhaps he has not always given the best sets of them, as he may not have had the good fortune to hear those sets . . . When he had frequent opportunities of hearing an air, he chose that set which appeared to him the best, the most genuine. When he had not such opportunities, he satisfied himself with writing the notes which he heard.[7]

There is an element of choice, of editing, in what the collector does. Vaughan Williams takes this one stage further, regarding his published versions of tunes as a further variant, and allowing himself to add or smooth out musical details: the long note before the last line of "O Little Town of Bethlehem," for example, is his invention. Mr. Garman of Forest Green didn't sing it like that.

This creative unreliability of the field collection comes vividly into focus when technology allowed collectors to start making sound-recordings around the beginning of the twentieth century. Thanks to the wonderful British Library sound archive, we can listen to the crackling sounds of men and women, some of whom watched as children when the lads of their village marched off to fight Boney, singing carols and slurping tea. Often, memories are remarkable. Sometimes melodies get muddled and songs stutter to a stop. Husbands and wives have a little bicker about what comes next. Regional accents can be completely impenetrable.

The fruits of these gleanings are priceless in every sense. As late as the 1970s, the great folklorist Roy Palmer was collecting variants of carols, and the stories to go with them, including the man who enjoyed going to the pub on Sunday afternoons in the 1940s, where he learned a local variant of "While Shepherds Watched" from a man called Bill, who was "a carpenter, but he didn't like work, Bill. He preferred to get his living by sleight of hand, and he avoided work like the plague." The story ends, "we used to go up there, and I started to learn to play the banjo. And then I met my wife, and I gave it up."[8] Of such is history.

So far, much of this has nothing to do with church. The liturgy, the content of divine worship, was prescribed by law and was no place for most of these irreverent impostors.

In the nineteenth century the church began to make a distinctive contribution of its own. The clergy played a crucial role as editors, translators, composers, arrangers, and authors. A number of familiar items were newly written in America. The stirring congregational tub-thumper and the organ to go with it were the invention of the Victorians.

Their successors, perhaps prudently, sought to ameliorate some of its excesses. The introduction to the *English Hymnal* of 1906 comments rather sniffily: "A large body of voices singing together makes a distinctly artistic effect, though that of each individual voice might be the opposite. And it may be added that a desire to parade a trained choir often accompanies a debased musical taste."[9] Clear echoes here of Sharp's reservations about the artistic value of the Christmas music in "fashionable churches."

Carol singing used to belong in the street far more than in the pew. The sight of carol singers merrily tramping from door to door has vanished to such an extent that we can easily forget just how familiar and widespread the practice was, until surprisingly recently. The carol used to be an outdoors creature, a farmyard animal as much as a domestic pet. Here's one account from 1869:

Having spent some part of my Christmas holidays in a retired little town in Gloucestershire, where many old customs and superstitions still linger, I of course came in for a good share of carol-singing. These, however, differed very much from the irreverent and discordant caterwauling (I cannot call it anything else) which greet our ears evening after evening in our suburban streets. For irreverent they could not well be, since sacred words were not attempted, and discordant they certainly were not, seeing that the singers were composed chiefly of the members of the choir.[10]

For all his *hauteur*, the writer captures well the types and sheer irrepressible ubiquity of *al fresco* singing in both town and country, and the carefree mixture of sacred and secular that forms the repertoire of these rude mechanicals.

Even as late as 1958, the hymnologist and carol historian Erik Routley can say that "there is no doubt that carol-singing is more popular and more widespread an activity in this country at the present time than it ever was before."[11] Wouldn't it be fun if we could learn to do this again?

And, still, the idea remains that a Christmas carol is in some respects a thing not quite proper for church. As late as 1971, Roy Palmer interviewed an elderly couple who sang him their local tune to "While Shepherds Watched."

"Where did you learn that?" Palmer asks.

"Round the streets. That was sung by carol-singers, when we went round collecting the pennies," is the reply. "But we never heard that sung in church. They're very traditional, in church."

"So, the church wouldn't have that?" asks Palmer.

"No, they just sing the ordinary 'While Shepherds Watched,' the thing out of the hymn book."[12]

You can hear the shock in her voice. The very idea.

At the same time, carols began to be considered worthy of academic attention. Early twentieth-century scholars put their texts in anthologies. The American linguist and philologist, Edith Rickert, included several hundred lyrics, meticulously sourced and edited, in her monumental 1910 publication *English Folk Carols 1400–1700* (though, in fact, her earliest examples are some two hundred years earlier than this). Rickert's introduction, helpfully classifying traditional carols into types, as Sylvester had done, is still a model of scholarship. Erik Routley wrote as well as anyone about the subject. His book is not as well known as it deserves. He is funny, humane, thoughtful, and the only writer man enough to acknowledge in print that "The First Nowell" is "really a rather terrible tune." Hear, hear.

Thanks to publications like the *English Hymnal*, the two "University" carol books and the *Cowley Carol Book*, the twentieth century came to value the inclusivity of a body of songs that everybody knew. The old distinction between indoor and outdoor carols was largely gone. Items that are more properly Christmas hymns are printed and sung alongside traditional Christmas carols. The editors of these books, like Luther, knew how to value a good tune, from wherever it comes, while still attempting to scrub off the remaining patina of "debased" Victorian sentimentality. The attempt continues.

Christmas carols are, perhaps, the nearest thing we still have to a folk tradition—an oral tradition. We know them because we know them. We never really learned them; they've just always been there. This gives the tradition a particularly fluid quality, able to absorb influences from all over the place, but never quite settling into a finished format.

How does the second verse of "O Little Town of Bethlehem" actually go? Or the last verse of "Away in a Manger"? Is it "stay by my side until morning is nigh" or "stay by my bedside till morning is nigh"? The poet must have written one or the other, surely?

Is there a passing note at "now in flesh ap-pea-ear-ring" or not? If not, why does everybody sing it? Should we try and stop them? How?

And, is it "Of the Father's *Heart* Begotten" or "*Love* Begotten"? At least when we're working with the published words of a well-known author we must be singing the words in an accepted, "correct" version, mustn't we? Well, no. Charles Wesley didn't write "Hark, the Herald Angels Sing," he wrote "Hark, How All the Welkin Rings." So why don't we sing it like that? Why do we sing carols in the versions we do? Because we just do. These tunes, gathered together like outcasts from all over the world, have taken on what Philip Larkin calls "the whiff of bands and organ-pipes and myrrh"[13] and taken their place around our festive table where children listen, ready to carry them on to the next generation and beyond.

When we sing our favorite carols at Christmas, we may think we're taking part in a long, unbroken, and unchanging tradition. This book shows the extent to which that is true, which is not very. There are lots of good stories and engaging characters, from the greatest musicians and thinkers to shepherd boys, choirboys, monks, and drunks. The best characters are the songs themselves, absorbed from their origins into the most profound and atavistic vein of Englishness. There is music. Some tunes you will know, and some you won't. There are some you might be surprised to find in a carol book ("On Ilkley Moor bah 'tat? Where's that?"). And there are lots more where these came from.

Enjoy exploring this unique and special part of our heritage.

Happy Christmas!

Advent

· 1 ·

"O Come, O Come Emmanuel"

 ome of our carols have become associated with celebrations of the birth of Jesus almost by accident. This one is bound into the liturgy and theology of Western Christianity since its earliest incarnations.

Its genesis lies in the "seven 'O's," the great Advent antiphons. These are a series of prayers each invoking Christ by one of the names or titles he is given in Scripture, ending with a supplication framed around that image. They are unimaginably ancient.

Boethius, the Roman author of *The Consolation of Philosophy* (whose writings about music gave medieval university students much grief) may show some familiarity with their language as far back as the early sixth century. The Anglo-Saxon poet Cynewulf wrote *The Christ* in about 750–800. Its first part, "Advent," movingly intersperses the gospel narrative of Mary and Joseph with a series of reflections that clearly echo the language and imagery of the great 'O's (the edition and translation here are Sir Israel Gollancz's, published in London in 1892):

Eala þu reccend and þu riht cyning
Se þe locan healdeð lif ontyneð
Eadga us siges oprum forwyrned
Wlitigan wil-sipes, gif his weorc ne deag.

O thou Ruler, and thou righteous King!
Thou Keeper of the keys that open life!
bless us with victory, with a bright career,
denied unto another, if his work is worthless!

2

The poem continues:

Eala earendel engla beorhtast
Ofer middan-geard monnum sended
And soðfæsta sunnan leoma,
Torht ofer tunglas. Þū tida gehwane
Of sylfum þe symle inlihtes.

Hail, heavenly beam, brightest of angels thou,
sent unto men upon this middle-earth!
Thou are the true refulgence of the sun,
radiant above the stars, and from thyself
illuminest for ever all the tides of time.

O thou God of spirits! how wisely thou
wast named, with name aright, Emmanuel!
as the angel spake the word in Hebrew first,
which in its secret meaning fully now
is thus interpreted: "The Guardian of the skies,
God's Self, is now with us."

(In passing, it was this edition that provided J. R. R. Tolkien with much of his imagery and several of his names, including Earendel and Middle Earth.)

Later in the first millennium those great crucibles of liturgical music, the powerhouse Benedictine monasteries of Northern France, employed the Abbot as cantor for the first of the 'O's, with each subsequent antiphon being intoned on successive days by the next most senior member of the establishment in descending order of importance (an interesting inverted pre-echo of the modern habit of having the "Nine Lessons" read in the opposite order of noteworthiness, the first by a nervous eight-year-old chorister trying to pretend he knows what a cicatrice is, then a student, right up to the local worthy).

Theologically, each antiphon links a prophecy of Isaiah through to its fulfillment in the gospel, echoing with the resonances of particular words and ideas through the Bible and beyond. Liturgically, the seven antiphons are sung before and after the Magnificat at Vespers on the last seven days of Advent (December 17–23). Remarkably, they survived and prospered into the Anglican and other Protestant traditions, though with some variation of the exact dates on which each is sung.

As with the gospels themselves, early Christian writers discovered (or created) several more to go with the original set. The basic set of seven each begin with the letter *O*, followed by the name or title being invoked: Sapientia; Adonai; Radix Jesse; Clavis David; Oriens; Rex Gentium; Emmanuel. Somebody noticed that the initial letters of these key words, if read in reverse order, spell the Latin phrase *Ero Cras*, and claimed that this meant "Tomorrow, I will come," in reference to the meaning of the season of Advent. Ingenious, but unlikely. For one thing, the phrase more accurately means "Tomorrow I will be," which is at best rather vague. For another, this sort of word play is not readily found in liturgical materials. Also, if it's a kind of hidden, coded prophecy building up to something, it spoils the point somewhat to do it backward. More likely, some clever monk in the Middle Ages, an era that thoroughly enjoyed its acrostics, word games, and number patterns, noticed the coincidence one bored day at Vespers and set that particular hare running.

The theological exegesis of the antiphons has occupied the minds of many brainy people. Perhaps we may allow ourselves one tentative toe in these learned waters to get some small idea of where the words and ideas of this carol come from.

The first antiphon begins *"O Sapientia, quae ex ore Altissimi prodisti . . . veni ad docendum nos viam prudentiae"* ("O Wisdom, proceeding from the mouth of the Highest . . . come and teach us the way of understanding"). Isaiah says, "The spirit of the Lord shall rest upon him, the spirit of wisdom and understanding." The Wisdom of Solomon has "wisdom reacheth from one end to another mightily: and sweetly doth she order all things." Joshua was "full of the spirit of wisdom." The child Jesus "grew, and waxed strong in spirit, filled with wisdom: and the grace of God was upon him." St. Paul asks "that the Father of glory, may give unto you the spirit of wisdom and revelation in the knowledge of him."[1]

The words are pregnant with the promise of fulfillment, like Advent itself. This is the promise the antiphons and their successor, the carol, seek to invoke.

The Advent antiphons are prose, with their own plainsong melody, and are still often sung by accomplished choirs. At some point they were versified into a regular meter and picked up a repeating refrain. The final stage was to marry them to an existing plainsong tune, originally intended for quite different words. A familiar classic emerges from the amalgamation of ancient, disparate elements.

Here is the Latin prose of the fourth antiphon:

O Clavis David, et sceptrum domus Israel: qui aperis, et nemo claudit; claudis, et nemo aperit: veni et educ vinctum de domo carceris, sedentem in tenebris, et umbra mortis.

(O key of David, and scepter of the House of Israel, who opens, and no man shuts; who shuts, and no man opens: come and lead from the prison house the captive who sits in darkness and in the shadow of death.)

And this is the metrical version, with its new refrain:

Veni, clavis Davidica!
Regna reclude caelica,
Fac iter tutum superum
Et claude vias inferum.
Gaude! Gaude! Emmanuel
Nascetur pro te, Israel.

The process by which the various versions merge and emerge is, of course, thoroughly hidden in the *tenebris* and the *umbra*. Finding a way through, introduces us to the work of unquestionably the two most important among the many Victorian clergymen in this story, John Mason Neale and Thomas Helmore.

Neale published the metrical Latin version, beginning "*Veni, veni, Emmanuel*," in 1851. He believed that it was written in the twelfth century, with the refrain being added at an unknown later date. This is entirely credible on stylistic grounds, though the earliest source known to Neale, and indeed since, is a Tridentine Catholic Psalter from Cologne, dating from 1710. He set another historical puzzle with his choice of tune, harmonized by Helmore. Neale told his readers it was "adapted from a French Missal." The secret of exactly what that meant was to wait another hundred years for its own advent out of darkness.

Translators and hymnologists soon started scurrying all over this hymn, with its stirring evocation of the themes of Advent and its unusual but memorable melody. One of the very first English versions of the original antiphons was written, fittingly, by none other than the Captain of the Catholics himself, John Henry Newman, in 1836. Editors and compilers followed with multiple translations of the hymn, using the same meter as the Latin so their words could be sung to the same tune.

These versions went forth and multiplied so enthusiastically that the strands of their individual verbal DNA have gotten completely muddled up and become totally indistinguishable, like fruit flies in a bell jar. Writers borrow words and phrases from each other, with and without acknowledgement. Some hymnbooks ascribe their version to Neale, ignoring (or not noticing) the fact that they have altered his very first line from "Draw nigh, draw nigh, Emmanuel" to "O come, O come, Emmanuel." Most give multiple attributions—to Neale, and Lacey, or the twelfth century, or Cologne, or anon, or unknown, or some combination of all these—usually adding the dreaded words "and Editors" or "and Compilers." Some think *Adonai* rhymes with *majesty*, others with *earth* and *sky*. How *do* you pronounce that word? Who knows? Modern choirs don't. And what is a *Dayspring*? And is it *Emmanuel* or *Immanuel*, which are at least pronounced the same?

It's probably impossible to know now exactly who first wrote what. Verses mysteriously change their order like the French in a bus queue.

Some assaults on the Latin, or bits of it, were committed by a person or persons unknown. It is enough, perhaps, for our purposes, to note that important contributions were made by, among many others, Neale, T. A. Lacey, and Henry Sloane Coffin. The version given at the end of this chapter is Neale's, as adapted by Coffin and used in *Hymns Ancient and Modern*.

One other version merits attention. In the 1850s, Neale and Helmore published their *Hymnal Noted*. This is No. 65:

The interesting point here is the proper plainsong notation (four-line stave, old-style clef, rhythmless "neumes" instead of crotchets and quavers, no bar lines), with English words. This is exactly what John Marbecke attempted at the Reformation. Respect the integrity of the old musical ways as much as possible, but give the people the words in their own language. The title of their hymnbook may well contain an echo of Marbecke's famous publication *The Booke of Common Praier Noted* of 1550. As scholars, Neale and Helmore were ahead of their time.

Other editors, of course, forced the tune into the straitjacket of a regular rhythmic pulse. It doesn't work. The tune won't go into 4/4, and arrangers have to keep chopping and changing their choice of time signature. All very confusing.

And what of the tune itself? Where did Neale get it from? *The Hymnal Noted* places the elusive French Missal, perhaps unexpectedly, in Lisbon. Neale spent the winter of 1853–1854 in Madeira, recuperating from a lung complaint brought on by living in Crawley (a curious coincidence with the medical history of Rev. Sabine Baring-Gould). He may have found his source on that trip. Others claim that it was Bishop Jenner who found the Lisbon book. Whatever the truth, the source text of Helmore's tune could not be found. Some even hinted that Helmore wrote the tune himself.

To get at the truth, we find ourselves in the excellent company of the eminent Cambridge-based plainsong scholar and nun, Mother Thomas More, aka Dr. Mary Berry. In 1966, Dr. Berry was on a research visit to France:

My attention had been drawn to a small fifteenth-century processional in the Paris Bibliothèque Nationale. It was Franciscan in origin and probably intended for the use of nuns rather than friars. Turning the pages I discovered, on folio 89v ff, a number of troped verses for the funeral responsory *Libera me* in the form of a litany, beginning with the words "Bone iesu, dulcis cunctis." The melody of these tropes was none other than the tune of "O come, O come Emmanuel." It appeared in square notation on the left-hand page, and on the opposite page there was a second part that fitted exactly, like a mirror-image, in note-against-note harmony with the hymn-tune. The book would thus have been shared by two sisters, each singing her own part as they processed. So it would seem that this great Advent hymn-tune was not, in the first instance, associated with Advent at all, but with a funeral litany . . . Perhaps it is a measure of Helmore's genius that he detected in this melody an appropriate Advent sound as well, one which conveys an unmistakable sense of solemn expectancy, not only for the Nativity of Christ, but also for his Second Coming . . . Helmore was shrewd enough, also, to have been aware that an indubitable link exists between the theology of Advent and a procession marking the passage from death to eternal life.[2]

It is just possible that Dr. Berry was looking at the same book wheezily pored over by Neale. More likely, another copy of the same chant made its way across Europe, perhaps within the Franciscan community, and ended up in Lisbon. Either way, we have our tune.

We have, too, probably our most ancient carol. Next time you use it to invoke the great promise of Advent, you are doing so in phrases and cadences that may not have sounded entirely unfamiliar to the earliest Christian musicians of all.

"O Come, O Come Emmanuel"

O come, Thou Rod of Jesse, free
Thine own from Satan's tyranny;
From depths of hell Thy people save,
And give them victory o'er the grave.
Refrain

O come, Thou Key of David, come,
And open wide our heavenly home;
Make safe the way that leads on high,
And close the path to misery.
Refrain

O come, Thou Day-Spring, come and cheer
Our spirits by Thine advent here;
Disperse the gloomy clouds of night
And death's dark shadows put to flight!
Refrain

O come, O come, Thou Lord of Might,
Who to Thy tribes on Sinai's height
In ancient times didst give the law
In cloud, and majesty, and awe.
Refrain

Feasting and Making Ready

"O, Christmas Tree"

ecause they are part of a folk tradition, some carols can exist in different versions in different places at the same time. "O, Christmas Tree" is better known today in America than in England. It got there with a little help from a family tree with many spreading branches of its own, including a Renaissance composer who lost his family in the Thirty Years' War, German students bellowing Latin songs into their beer, and a nineteenth-century poet and church organist. Among its cousins are an Irish revolutionary honored by Lenin, the state of Maryland, Manchester United football club, and the British Labour Party. Christmas carols have roots and offshoots in all sorts of unlikely places.

To some, "O, Christmas Tree" may not count as a carol at all. The words are a translation of a German poem beginning "O Tannenbaum," but a Tannenbaum isn't specifically a Christmas tree, it's just a fir tree. Apart from this bit of creative mistranslation, the poem makes no reference to Christmas at all, and certainly not to anything remotely connected with the Christian story. The tree is used as an image of reliability and changelessness in a fleeting world. Also, the poem's status as a translation shows perhaps more clearly than any other Christmas song how an oral, rather than a composed, tradition never settles into a final form. Nobody knows what the "correct" version is, because there isn't one.

The Internet provides the perfect vehicle for revealing how this kind of dissemination by Chinese whispers works. Do a web search for the words of this song and you'll find, among much else, people looking for "the words I knew in childhood," finding something a bit like what they remember but not quite, and asking if anyone out there knows the rest of the ones that go something like

O Christmas Tree, O Christmas Tree
How lovely are thy branches
O Christmas Tree, O Christmas Tree
How dum de dum dum dum dum
La la la laaaa, in summertime
La la la laaaa, in wintertime.
O Christmas tree, etc.

Replies are many and various, but none quite matches the questioner's memory. The past is a foreign country—they do things differently there. Recorded versions have all sorts of different sets of lyrics. Versions by artists as potent as Aretha Franklin and Alvin and the Chipmunks are alike in their basic theme and their key features, but quite dissimilar in detail.

Does it matter? Not a bit. This is what an oral tradition is.

The tune, on the other hand, first appeared in print in 1824, with the name of a perfectly sensible composer attached. It, surely, must be safe from being mangled by the funny tricks of time, at least as far as important details like the number of beats in a bar are concerned? Well, no. Never mind whether the pairs of quavers are dotted or not, beneath the swooping strings and mooing horns under which this poor, innocent little melody is so often buried, you can find versions with four beats to the bar instead of three.

Should we be surprised? Should we be bothered? Not really. When something like a tune is passed on by memory and by performance, it will both change and stay the same. The same is true of language. That's how it evolves. "Happy Birthday to You" started out in 4/4 time, and now it's in 3/4.

So, the version given at the end of this chapter is the tune as first published in 1824, to the harmony given in the Yale songbook, with one of the more common current English translations.

We pick up the story beneath a castle overlooking the river Itz, in Bavaria, in the dangerous days of the early seventeenth century and the composer Melchior Franck. Franck lived through a period of musical transition. His huge output (six hundred motets and many other works) combines the old-fashioned sound world of Renaissance composers like Lassus with the new polychoral style brought over the mountains from Venice, and local experiments like fugue and *basso continuo*. As well as his many "learned" compositions, Franck also wrote songs. In one of them, he taps into an already well-established tradition in praising the humble and ubiquitous fir tree as an emblem of the natural world's comforting reliability and predictability, so unlike the world of men. And well he might. The area around Coburg, where he lived, was devastated by the violence and the political and economic degradation of the Thirty Years' War. Many musicians lost their livelihoods. Returning armies brought typhus to the streets. Franck's wife and two of his children died.

Franck's words begin *"Ach Tannebaum, ach Tannebaum, du bist ein edler Zweig! Du grünest uns den Winter, die lieben Sommerzeit."* The "noble branch" stays green through summer and winter. Franck did not invent the idea of singing to a tree; versions of the lyric exist as far back as 1550, six decades earlier. His poem is not the beginning of the story; it's a staging post.

Medieval German students liked singing Latin songs. As with most things students do, they were sometimes regarded with a degree of disapproval, as Brahms found to his cost when he incorporated *Gaudeamus igitur* ("Let us therefore make merry") into his "Academic Festival Overture," apparently not a very academic thing to do. One of these songs begins

Lauriger Horatius, quam dixisti verum:
Fugit Euro citius tempus edax rerum!

The laureled Horace is hymned for his willingness to kiss the girl, drink the wine, defy the tyrant time slipping through his fingers and generally *carpe diem*. No wonder cloistered academics find themselves dabbing feebly at a disapproving brow.

As usual, it is far from clear where this lyric comes from. It appears in print at the end of the eighteenth century, but it is impossible to be certain if it had been around for some time or had just been newly written. Naturally enough, the song then became a staple of student songbooks. It features regularly in editions of the celebrated "Yale" songbook from 1858. From there, having entered the United States, it goes on to become associated with other words, including the state song "Maryland, My Maryland."

How did this tune get hitched to all these words, and what on earth has it all got to do with fir trees? Like the words, the tune is a creature with its origins in folk traditions and has passed through many hands and incarnations. It seems to first appear in print at the very end of the eighteenth century, to yet another German text, "Es lebe Hock." It appears without words in another printed collection at around the same time. Both appear to be based on the "Lauriger Horatius" tune, which is itself probably a version of a Westphalian folk song. So, both tune and words are part of a process of evolution from hazy folk traditions into something approaching the form we know today. They first got together shortly after the tune first appeared in print.

Ernst Anschütz was a teacher, organist, poet, and composer. He spent his whole life in Leipzig, plying his various trades there for fifty years. His poems were set as lieder, and he wrote the libretto for a singspiel by Carl Loewe as well as an account of the death of the soldier Johann Woyzeck, later turned into a play by Georg Büchner and thence into an opera by Alban Berg.

In 1824, Anschütz wrote and published a song, "O Tannenbaum, o Tannenbaum, Wie treu sind deine Blätter!" with a tune that is a simple piano harmonization of the familiar "Lauriger Horatius" melody. The carol we know today is born. Sort of.

But we still can't quite claim that we have our author, still less our composer. Anschütz hadn't written the first verse, he had taken it from a version published just a few years earlier by August Zarnack, who, in turn, may well have based it on another version of the folk lyric, beginning "O Dannebom," another name for the modest little fir tree. Zarnack had turned the imagery of the tree's constancy into a song about a faithless lover, which meant Anschütz had to edit its first verse slightly to fit with his second and third verses. Subsequent verses may not be by Anschütz either, though it's not clear who, if anyone, did write them. As is so often the case with these carols, Anschütz's role was to join together strands from all sorts of existing traditions. He did a good job. From here the song spreads its branches across the world with the growing popularity of the Christmas tree itself, famously popularized in England by another German import, Prince Albert.

During the rest of the nineteenth century, the song takes its hallowed place around the domestic Christmas hearth. The English novelist Maria Singleton wrote in 1865:

> Joyously did the little ones form a circle around that magic tree; and gleefully rang their voices as they saluted it in the well-known strains of that ancient song:

> O Christmas tree! O Christmas tree!
> How lovely are thy branches![1]

In 1879 John McElroy notes its popularity in America, calling the tune "old, and a familiar one to all college students." He gives part of a "fine" translation by Longfellow, beginning "Oh hemlock tree," and points out that the "Oh Maryland" variant began as a rebel song before the Civil War.[2] It is not the last time the tune is to be co-opted by the forces of violent revolution.

Irving Bacheller's 1911 novel *Keeping Up with Lizzie* puts the tune to rather more peaceful use:

> I was to dine with the Warburtons Christmas Eve, and be Santa Claus for the children . . . The little captain of three years ran straight to Mrs. Bill an' lay hold of her gown, an' partly hid himself in its folds, an' stood peekin' out at me . . . She raised him in her arms an' held him close. A great music-box in a corner began to play:

"O tannenbaum! O tannenbaum! wie grun sind deine blaetter!"
Well, it was the night of my life.[3]

Typically, printing lags behind oral transmission. English versions of the song first appear in print in the first decade of the twentieth century, after which it becomes a regular feature of household songbooks and carol collections. In 1914, the song once again reaches out from Germany to the English-speaking world in the famous Christmas truce of that year, when, according to one soldier's diary, "They all began clapping; and then they struck up another favourite of theirs, 'O Tannenbaum.' And so it went on. First the Germans would sing one of their carols and then we would sing one of ours."[4]

The tune has the memorable simplicity necessary for lasting popularity: four lines; lines one, two, and four all the same (a feature of so many familiar tunes); line three a simple downward sequence. Sing it once and you know it forever. Its opening rhythm makes it eminently suitable for singing to all kinds of different words, as many budding wordsmiths have noticed. Any three-syllable name with a "tum-te-tum" rhythm will do, from Field-Marshal von Hindenburg to the Manchester United goalkeeper Edwin van der Sar: "Oh, Van der Sar, oh, Van der Sar, we'll always love you where you are."

American place-names fit particularly well: "Oh, Maryland, my Maryland" or Florida or Albany or Michigan . . . you get the idea. "The Red Flag" is a revolutionary lyric by the Irish nationalist Jim Connell. Connell had wanted it sung to an old Jacobite tune, but it, too, got itself stuck to the "Tannenbaum" tune, becoming the unofficial anthem of the British Labour Party.

The image of green shoots in the depth of winter is older than Christianity. This song, like so many, taps into something all the more profound for being unfathomably ancient. It is part of who we are. Yet, like us, and like the imagery we use to describe ourselves to ourselves, it has changed continually, and changes still.

"O, Christmas Tree"

O Christmas Tree, O Christmas Tree,
What happiness befalls me
O Christmas Tree, O Christmas Tree,
What happiness befalls me
When oft at joyous Christmas-time
Your form inspires my song and rhyme.
O Christmas Tree, O Christmas Tree,
What happiness befalls me.

O Christmas Tree, O Christmas Tree,
Your boughs can teach a lesson
O Christmas Tree, O Christmas Tree,
Your boughs can teach a lesson
That constant faith and hope sublime
Lend strength and comfort through all time.
O Christmas Tree, O Christmas Tree,
Your boughs can teach a lesson.

· 3 ·

"The Holly and the Ivy"

Holly standeth in the hall fair to behold,
Ivy stands without the door; she is full sore a-cold. (anon)

Deck the hall with boughs of holly. (Thomas Oliphant, English
    version of words to a Welsh New Year Carol)

Heigh ho! sing heigh ho! unto the green holly:
Most friendship is feigning, most loving mere folly:
Then, heigh ho! the holly!
This life is most jolly. (Shakespeare)

Now the holly bears a berry as red as the blood. (anon)

Green grow'th the holly
So doth the ivy
Though winter blasts blow never so high
Green grow'th the holly. (Henry VIII)

Down with the holly, ivy, all
Wherewith ye dress'd the Christmas hall. (Herrick)

n song, like in the garden, ivy gets everywhere. So doth the
holly.
The potency of the imagery is clear. The shiny green leaves

and bright red berries brandish a powerful message of new life in the dark, midwinter wood. It's a short step to the image of the Christ-child. Throw in all the mentions of cherries and berries, mistletoe and yew, juniper and box, and our Christmas tradition really does become, as a Dutch carol has it, *"een hofken, er schoon bloemkens staen"* ("a garden full of divers flowers").

The humble holly bush and creeping ivy take their place among some of the oldest and strangest imagery in our collective lyrical memory, where the cycles of the natural world meet Christian ideas of birth, life, and death. Here, too, are the three ravens paying court to the dead knight and the fallow doe "As great with yong as she might goe," and the predatory falcon of the "Corpus Christi Carol" ("lully, lullay, the falcon hath borne my make away"). The eyes of these creatures still peer at us from under our not-quite-made bed of modern civilization.

A recurring idea in the songs of the holly and the ivy is the competition between them for preeminence ("of all the trees that are in the wood, the holly bears the crown"; "Nay ivy, nay, it shall not be, i-wys, Let holly have the mastery as the manner is"; "the first tree in the greenwood, it was the holly"). Sometimes this takes the form of a wooing song or mating ritual, the holly representing the boy, the ivy the girl (and the holly always comes out on top, from which we will avert our attention with some relief).

Their deep roots in this kind of imagery make these songs the perfect examples of how ancient, pagan ideas have become assimilated, though not fully absorbed, into Christian iconography. The church, naturally enough, has not always been happy about making houseroom for superstition and secular merry-making. That favorite old celebrity St. Nicholas, for example, carried all sorts of unwelcome associations in his sack: the Lords of Misrule, the ceremony of the Boy-Bishop, and Twelfth Night Revels. All good fun, but definitely not textbook Christian practice. In London, on December 5, 1554, "the which was saint Nicholas' eve, at evensong time, came a commandment that saint Nicholas should not go abroad, nor about. But, notwithstanding, there went about these St. Nicholases, in divers parishes."[1] Folk traditions are as tenacious as ivy. Much later, Cecil Sharp is making the argument in reverse, defending traditional songs against incursions by Christians, and sticking up for "the unconscious art of the peasant" before "his carols suffered from the intrusion of theological doctrine."[2] Holly and ivy certainly received their share of such proselytizing attentions, welcome or otherwise.

Some of these holly and ivy songs do not attempt to link their imagery to the Christian story at all. "The contest of the holly and the ivy," for example, assigns various characteristics to each plant, or links them to some other species such as birds (the "laverock" for the holly, the owl for the ivy). The masculine/feminine duality runs throughout:

> Holly and his merry men, they dancen and they sing;
> Ivy and her maidens, they weepen and they wring.

"The Holly and the Ivy" and its close cousin "The Sans-Day Carol," by contrast, compare various aspects of Christ's life and ministry with some botanical peculiarity, often using a color to symbolize the scriptural reference—red for Christ's blood, white for his burial shroud:

> The holly bears a berry as red as any blood,
> And Mary bore sweet Jesus Christ to do poor sinners good.
>   ("The Holly and the Ivy")

> Now the holly bears a berry as white as the milk,
> And Mary bore Jesus who was wrapped up in silk. ("The Sans-
>   Day Carol")

Verses, of course, vary between versions. A number appeared in print in the century or so from about 1810.[3] Cecil Sharp got his version from Mrs. Clayton of Chipping Camden, which he "supplemented" with parts of a slightly different text sung by Mrs. Wyatt of East Harptree in Somerset. Sharp also changed Mrs. Clayton's "obviously incorrect" last line of verse two ("On Christmas Day in the morn") to match the version printed by, among others, Stainer, Sylvester, and the Birmingham ballad seller Wadsworth.

Incorrect, or a local variant?

Thus do Sharp, Clayton, Wyatt, and Wadsworth all serve their function as editors of the text we have today.

The refrain of this carol really needs to be considered separately. It doesn't quite fit. For one thing, the imagery suddenly takes a lurch inside. Up to now, we have been entirely out in the woods, among the bushes and briars. We stay there for the first two lines of the refrain, watching the sun rise and the deer run. Then, suddenly, we're in church, listening to an organ and a choir. It's an odd change of gear.

Also, an organ is a man-made thing. The word, in its meaning of a machine with pipes kept indoors, dates from the Middle Ages. The phrase "merry organ" is used by Chaucer. Compared to the rest of the text, the reference is bizzarely modern. For all its relevance to holly, ivy, blood, and thorns, our caroler might as well have told us he's switched on his iPod.

And it doesn't scan. The first two lines don't match the verses, and the last two lines don't match the first two lines. "The playing of the merry organ" just won't fit the tune, whatever metrical and musical contortions ballad singers, editors, and arrangers have put it through over the years.

It doesn't rhyme, either.

Is this refrain actually part of the same poem? Has it at some point been altered from a metrically unexceptionable but theologically unsound original?

There is probably a remnant here of an attempt to Christianize the lyric a little further than it really wanted to go. It's possible, also, that the refrain was appended at a later date to an existing poem, and that what we now know as verse one originally functioned as the refrain. This would explain the change of gear.

There is another line of inquiry.

Overleaf are two ballad broadsides. Both were printed in Birmingham in the second and third decades of the nineteenth century (the first may be the earlier). They are among the earliest printed sources of this carol.

Look carefully at the words of the refrain.

The second broadside (right) has "the playing of the merry organ," as expected. The first (left) has "the playing of the merry groan."

The merry what?

Is this a mistake? Is it a coincidence that *groan* is an anagram of *organ*? Did a careless printer or feckless printer's lad, thinking about football or his girlfriend instead of concentrating on his job, muddle up the metal letters as he hammered them into place, ready for inking? Was he dyslexic? Did someone proofread it for him and get it wrong, an early instance of the curse of the spell-checker?

There is another possibility. *Groan* might be correct. Is it a musical instrument, a slang or vernacular term, perhaps, for some kind of bag-pipe or "drone," or a drum?

It's an immensely appealing theory. It makes the line scan perfectly. *Groan* is a half-rhyme for *sun* (perhaps more than half in Birmingham). And what a fabulous picture it conjures up: our caroling ancestor dancing round the holly-bush in the moonlight, swigging his ale, singing this song, and playing the groan. It doesn't matter whether we have any idea what a groan actually is or not. Just imagine it. Hear the sound of the merry groan. Good, isn't it?

The tune, unlike the words, has not undergone much metamorphosis. Apart from editors fiddling with the rhythms in an effort to get their particular choice of words to fit, the melody doesn't change between versions. It can't, really: it's a simple little thing. Hints of possible ways to sing it might be gleaned from the phrase-structure of the music itself. The distinctive rising major sixth in the first two lines makes it work particularly well as a round, sung at three beats' distance, like pealing bells (perhaps working best if the round stops after two lines of text). There are lots of rounds in folk music and children's songs. It's a great way to create instant harmony and make a song last longer.

To take this idea a little further, the text of "The Sans-Day Carol" is so similar to "The Holly and the Ivy" that it almost, in some respects, sounds like a smartened-up version of the traditional original. Also, the two tunes can, almost, be sung together. Did one begin life as a sort of counter-melody or descant to the other? Or an alternative answering melody in a round? It would not be the only instance of such a process in English folk song.

There is one alternative tune to these words, completely different in character, usually described as an Old French melody. It appears in print a number of times between 1870 and 1930, including in Stainer's collection. It hasn't remained in use, however, perhaps because the French flavor of the tune does not really match the feel and rhythm of the words (and makes even less effort to accommodate the pesky spare syllable inserted by the merry organist).

If "The Holly and the Ivy" has a theological point, it's less to do with the nativity than with what the nativity led on to. Not so much that "Mary bore sweet Jesus Christ" but that he came "to do poor sinners good." Wedding these words solely to Christmas was always a marriage of convenience that never quite succeeded in covering up some basic differences between the two partners, though it's been going strong for a good while now.

And alongside the theology, of course, is a strong dose of the use of holly and ivy as decorations for the midwinter hall and home in the dark days around the solstice. Like the carol, the trees themselves look on toward Easter and spring:

> The holly hitherto did sway;
> Let box now domineer,
> Until the dancing Easter-day,
> Or Easter's eve appear.[4]

"The Holly and the Ivy"

The holly bears a blossom as white as any flower,
And Mary bore sweet Jesus Christ to be our sweet saviour.
Refrain

The holly bears a berry as red as any blood,
And Mary bore sweet Jesus Christ to do poor sinners good.
Refrain

The holly bears a prickle as sharp as any thorn,
And Mary bore sweet Jesus Christ on Christmas Day in the morn.
Refrain

The holly bears a bark as bitter as any gall,
And Mary bore sweet Jesus Christ for to redeem us all.
Refrain

The Journey to Bethlehem

"I Saw Three Ships"

lenty of carols mix and match elements from all parts of the Christian story. Few give the mixture quite such an enthusiastic shake as this one. The results, when you look closely, are a little odd.

Our narrator watches ships sailing into Bethlehem, which is landlocked and twenty miles from the nearest river. There are three ships and two passengers. The adult Jesus never did enter into Bethlehem. Mary only did so before his birth.

It seems that, in this instance, several stories and aspects of stories have been piped aboard the good ship *"Carol"* and sent sailing off round the musical world, picking up acquaintances and making friends among the indigenous population as they go. The associations of this song are rich and strange. Christ and his mother are compared to many things in medieval iconography: a shepherd, a pelican, a warrior; the sun, a pearl, the star of the sea. Sailors, not often. There are many layers of meaning beneath the sparkling surface of our seasonal sea-shanty, some sunk too deep for us to fathom now.

Our guides in these great waters are the men who wrote down and printed the song as it appeared to them.

The first is a seventeenth-century Scot named John Forbes. Forbes published his *Cantus, Songs and Fancies to Three, Four or Five Parts* in "Aberdene" in 1666. He begins with an impressively thorough course in music theory, as taught by his friend Thomas Davidson at the local music school ("Q. What is imperfect tyme? A. Two semi-briefs to the brief").

His contents show Scotland lagging some half a century behind the old enemy to the south in musical taste and accomplishment (no surprise, perhaps, given the events of recent decades). Here are songs by Dowland, Campion, and Morley, ornaments of the Elizabethan and Jacobean court in London and long since dead. Restoration jollity has not reached Aberdene. There is one vigorously Scottish ploughing (or *pleughing*) song with its ritual naming of the beasts: Higgin and Habken, Hankin and Rankin, Philpie Foster and Macky Millar, Straboots, Tarboyes and Ganzel. Sacred and secular rub shoulders unremarked, as usual.

CANTUS,

Songs and Fancies,

To Three, Four, or
Five Parts,

Both apt for Voices and Viols.

With a brief Introduction
to Musick,

*As is taught by Thomas
Davidson, in the Musick-
School of Aberdene.*

Second Edition, Corrected
and Enlarged.

A B E R D E N E,
Printed by JOHN FORBES, and are to be sold at his shop,
Anno Domini. M. DC. LXVI.

And are to be sold at EDINBURGH by DAVID TRENCH, Book-seller.

Then comes the song, reproduced overleaf.

The words repay reading with some care.

We begin with the sons of Adam, then a hymn to the Trinity. Then we hear the message of the angel at the Annunciation. Then, curiously, we're on board a ship, steered by the Archangel Michael, St. John (the Evangelist, presumably) in the prow (or *horn*), Christ playing the

LL fones of Adam, rife up with me, Go praife the bleffed Trinitie.
Go

Go praife the bleffed Trinitie.　Cry Kyrie, with Hofanna,　fing Alleluja now.

Save us all, Emanuel.　Then fpake th'Archangel Gäbriel, faid, "Ave Mary mild,

the Lord of Lords is with thee, now fhal you go with child : *Ecce ancilla Do-*

mini.　Then faid the Vir - gin,　As thou haft faid, fo mat it be,　ij

Welcom be heavens King,　welcom be heavens King.　There comes a fhip far

failing then, Saint Michel was the ftieres-man: Saint Iohn fate in the horn : Our
K 2　　　　　　　　　　　　　　　　　　　　　　Lord

Lord harped, our Lady fang, And all the bells of heaven they rang, On Chrifts

Sunday at morn, On Chrifts Sonday at morn. Then fang the Angels all & fome,

Lauda Deum tuum, Si -　on. The fons of Adam anfwered, then fang,

Glore be to the God and man, the Father and the Sprite, Alfo with honor

and perpetual joy, with honor and perpetual joy.

harp, Mary singing, bells ringing for a festival identified as "Christ's Sunday" (a delicious phrase, with perhaps more resonance of Easter than Christmas). Angels sing. The sons of Adam answer.

It's a lovely poem. The rhyme scheme is elegant and fluid. Lines and phrases are repeated at the ends of sections to gently emphasize the message of calm joy. The image of the ship takes its place in a shifting, kaleidoscopic overview of scenes from the lives of Christ and the saints. Liturgically, we are nowhere and everywhere. When would we sing Kyrie, Alleluia, and Hosanna all at the same time? The figure of Christ appears first as a promise on the lips of the angel, then, without pause for breath, as a grown man playing the harp. Something similar happens in "The Cherry-Tree Carol" too. Folk song meets liturgical ritual, with the usual results. A beautiful muddle.

The next source is much later, in 1833. In between, the lyric has lost some of its associations and gained some new ones. The two Archangels (whose festivals are part of the background hinterland of our Christmas celebrations) have gone ashore. In their place, we have picked up a first-person narrator.

Many carols use the first person plural ("Here we come a-wassailing," "We wish you a merry Christmas," "therefore we moun singen Deo Gracias"), betraying roots in the groups of carolers tramping from door to door in search of cheer, beer, cheese, and sweeties. The singular form is more a thing of poems and lyrics of the fifteenth century and earlier, more suited to the solitary young man with just his lute for company, singing to the Virgin Mary ("I saw a maiden sitten and sing," "I cry to thee, thou hear to me," "Nay, ivy, nay, it shall not be i-wys," "I sing of a maiden that is makeless"). It's an unusual feature. Our singular narrator brings resonances from a number of traditions and legends to bear.

The editor of the 1833 source was William Sandys. He knew Forbes's text from a book of *Scotch Songs* compiled by a collector called Ritson, and quoted it in his introduction. He also knew several English variants of the carol, in addition to the one he printed.

There are lots. Many surfaced in the century after Sandys. The plot remains roughly the same. The narrator sits at his ease, watching as part of the Gospel narrative of Christmas unfolds before his lazy eyes. A common variant begins:

As I sat on a sunny bank,
A sunny bank,
A sunny bank,
As I sat on a sunny bank
On Christmas Day in the morning.

Sometimes he sits "under a sycamore tree" or "at my cottage door." An interesting plot twist is that the itinerant mariners are often not Mary and Jesus, but Mary and Joseph. Sometimes we meet them on the way to the scene of the nativity, Mary "with child," sometimes on the way back, celebrating and giving thanks. In one, we watch from a Kentish cliff top as they sail up the English Channel. In another, also set in Kent or Sussex, they are on their way to be taxed. (In Dover? This transplanting of Gospel narrative to the green and pleasant fields of England is an interesting echo of the popular myth that Joseph of Arimathea brought Jesus himself to these islands, a story immortalized by Blake in his lyric "And did those feet in ancient time / Walk upon England's mountains green," written at about the same time as Sandys assembled his book of carols. Shakespeare mentions it too.)

There are secular versions, too, appropriately enough from seafaring towns. Sir Cuthbert Sharpe, Collector of Customs at Sunderland and Newcastle-upon-Tyne, noted this (and its tune, a variant of our main melody) in the first part of the nineteenth century:

I saw three ships come sailing in . . .
On New Year's Day in the morning.

And what do you think was in them then? . . .
Three pretty girls were in them then.

Another change in the centuries between Forbes and Sandys is that the bells are now ringing on earth, not in heaven. Mary and Joseph join in, though they appear to have left Jesus's harp in Scotland:

> He did whistle, and she did sing,
> And all the bells on earth did ring.

A noisy carol, this one.

The story has absorbed another important influence too. Forbes mentions only one ship. By the time Sandys wrote the song down in 1833, there are three. A much-quoted explanation for this lies in the legend of the "Kings of Cologne." These mythical monarchs are none other than the magi, or wise men, who brought gifts to the infant Jesus. Sir Thomas Browne, writing in 1646, tells us how they are supposed to have got to Germany: "[A]bout three hundred years after (Christ), by Helena the Empress, their bodies were translated to Constantinople, thence by Eustatius into Milan, and at last, by Renatus the Bishop, into Cologne (1170), where they are believed at present to remain, their monuments shown unto strangers, and having lost their Arabian titles, are crowned Kings of Cologne."[1]

Scripture, of course, nowhere says that the wise men were three in number, only that between them they brought three gifts. But legend (and Origen) has made them three, and given them names, and, as befits their status, they get a ship each. The townspeople line the banks of the Rhine, watching the stately progress of the sacred flotilla through their town, on its way to their enormous new cathedral ready to receive its consecrated cargo, prepared for the pilgrims who will pay homage to these brand-new antiques (and pay the inn-keepers and brothel-keepers of Cologne too). Word spreads across Europe. The striking image of the three ships gets hitched to an English folk tune or country dance. Over time, through constant repetition and embellishment, the defunct wise men get shoved overboard, their place taken by members of the Holy Family in various combinations. Three ships, two passengers.

Forbes also mentions the Trinity. Is there a residual echo of this reference in the number of ships? The number three has many echoes.

Sandys's edition of this carol provided the principal source for most carol books since. His, therefore, is basically the version we have used ever since, and still do.

Here it is:

Notice anything odd? Sandys has chosen to notate the song in 3/4 time. It clearly isn't. It would be tempting to posit some learned theory about a coded reference to the number three and the "bleffed Trinitie," the sort of thing a mathematically minded medieval musician would have enjoyed squirreling away in his scores for future generations to pore over.

Alas, the truth is probably more prosaic. Sandys wasn't a great musician. Some of his harmonies and bass-lines are noticeably clunky. Carol historian Erik Routley thinks his harmonizations sound like "Auntie at the parlour piano."[2] Bar lines often don't go with word-stress. Look at his version of "The Cherry-Tree Carol" ("Joseph was an old man"), which has an engaging wonky charm to its rhythm, and a big fat accent on the words *an* and *of.* And (whisper it not in Askelon), has anyone spotted the parallel fifths and octaves?

It's a mistake. No other edition follows his choice of time signature. Sandys hadn't read Forbes on the difference between "perfect and imperfect tyme."

In the decades after Sandys, many editors and compilers found this little thing irresistible, including Rimbault, Stainer, and Terry. It became, or remained, immensely popular. William Henry Husk wrote in 1868: "It is found, under various forms, in nearly every collection of sheet carols."[3] The indispensable Cecil Sharp collected many versions, often of the "As I sat on a sunny bank" variety. In a touching Christmas scene in her 1880 novel *Jack and Jill*, Louisa May Alcott quotes a rather sanitized version by the children's author Mary Mapes Dodge:

What shall little children bring
On Christmas Day, on Christmas Day?
What shall little children bring
On Christmas Day in the morning?

The grand old carols they shall sing
On Christmas Day, on Christmas Day;
With all their hearts, their offerings bring
On Christmas Day in the morning[4]

Sharp and others occasionally heard the carol sung to alternative tunes, as is to be expected, and one of these tunes made its way into a couple of published collections. But none ever seriously challenged Sandys's tune in the affections of carolers at large.

William Sandys preserved and recorded many of our best-loved carols. His editions placed them firmly and permanently in the popular consciousness. He probably wouldn't have passed Grade V theory, but without him, and his contemporaries and successors as collectors and compilers, Christmas would be quieter, not so tuneful, less rich in shared memory, and nothing like as much fun.

"I Saw Three Ships"

And what was in those ships all three?
On Christmas day, on Christmas day,
And what was in those ships all three?
On Christmas day in the morning.

Our Saviour Christ and his lady
On Christmas day, on Christmas day,
Our Saviour Christ and his lady,
On Christmas day in the morning.

Pray whither sailed those ships all three?
On Christmas day, on Christmas day,
Pray whither sailed those ships all three?
On Christmas day in the morning.

Oh, they sailed into Bethlehem,
On Christmas day, on Christmas day,
Oh, they sailed into Bethlehem,
On Christmas day in the morning.

And all the bells on earth shall ring,
On Christmas day, on Christmas day,
And all the bells on earth shall ring,
On Christmas day in the morning.

And all the Angels in Heaven shall sing,
On Christmas day, on Christmas day,
And all the Angels in Heaven shall sing,
On Christmas day in the morning.

And all the souls on earth shall sing,
On Christmas day, on Christmas day,
And all the souls on earth shall sing,
On Christmas day in the morning.

Then let us all rejoice, amain,
On Christmas day, on Christmas day,
Then let us all rejoice, amain,
On Christmas day in the morning.

December 24: Christmas Eve

"O Little Town of Bethlehem"

he hymn we know as "O Little Town of Bethlehem" contains ingredients from two completely different traditions, mixed together by a representative of a third.

The words are by a nineteenth-century American bishop, Phillips Brooks. The tune is an English folk song. The credit for the idea of combining them belongs to one of England's greatest composers, Ralph Vaughan Williams, a man passionately committed to the musical history and traditions of his country, undertaking the entirely practical job of assembling a hymnbook that people would actually want to use. He succeeded brilliantly.

Phillips Brooks was born in Massachusetts in 1836. He was sacked from his first job, remarking a little later "my only ambition is to be a parish priest."[1] Ordained in 1860, his imposing character and gifts as a leader created many demands beyond ministry to his large and loyal congregations, most of which he turned down. He did, however, lecture at his *alma mater*, Harvard, and became Bishop of Massachusetts in 1891. When he died, little more than a year later, the city of Boston "buried him like a king . . . a great man had fallen in Israel."[2]

His monument is the church he built. Trinity Church is a true sermon in stone, its text the life and witness of a particular breed of late-nineteenth-century Anglican clergymen. Its massive, redbrick bulk roots it firmly in the history of the city clustered around it: the balcony where Sam Adams read the Declaration of Independence to his fellow citizens; the harbor that staged the Boston Tea Party; Boston Common, where Paul Revere mustered his ragbag troop; Bunker Hill, where patriots fought and died. The church itself drips with "the beauty of holiness": the Venetian mosaics; windows by William Morris and Edward Burne-Jones; the first free-standing liturgical altar in the United States; choir stalls for the kind of "thrilling music" he heard on a visit to Rome; and Brooks himself, six foot four of zealotry in stone, arm raised, Bible in hand, robes flowing behind him. Oxford comes to Boston.

Brooks could write. Listen to the rolling cadences of his funeral oration for Abraham Lincoln, delivered in a sonorous, patrician New England accent, yards from where Lincoln's body lay in Independence Hall, Philadelphia:

> One brave, reckless man came forth to cast himself, almost single-handed, with a hopeless hope, against the proud power that he hated, and trust to the influence of a soul marching on into the history of his countrymen to stir them to a vindication of the truth he loved: . . . the swarthy multitudes came in, ragged, and tired, and hungry, and ignorant, but free forever from anything but the memorial scars of the fetters and the whip, singing rude songs in which the new triumph of freedom struggled and heaved below the sad melody that had been shaped for bondage . . . But slavery will not die . . . while one man counts another man his born inferior for the colour of his skin . . . So let him lie here in our midst today . . . this best and most American of all Americans . . . May God make us worthy of the memory of Abraham Lincoln![3]

This is the kind of preaching that echoes down the years into the world of Martin Luther King, Jr., and beyond. Thrilling stuff.

Like his English counterparts, Brooks was devoted to the idea of congregational hymn singing. And his congregations deserved the best he could give. Here, he experiments with an unusual five-line scheme:

> The earth has grown old with its burden of care,
> But at Christmas it always is young,

The heart of the jewel burns lustrous and fair,
And its soul full of music breaks forth on the air,
When the song of the Angels is sung.

This goes one line further:

The silent stars are full of speech
For who hath ears to hear;
The winds are whispering each to each,
The moon is calling to the beach,
And stars their sacred lessons teach
Of Faith, and Love, and Fear.

Brooks knew his Tennyson and his Matthew Arnold (and perhaps the T. S. Eliot of "Prufrock" knew his Brooks).

Brooks wrote carols for Easter too. This one has the seventeenth-century simplicity of the language that landed with the *Mayflower*, just down the coast, the Puritan directness of Richard Baxter and the *Bay Psalm-Book*:

God hath sent His Angels
To the earth again,
Bringing joyful tidings
To the sons of men.

They who first at Christmas
Thronged the heavenly way,
Now beside the tomb-door
Sit on Easter-Day.

The most famous lyric in this collection is the first. Like the others, it is illustrated with a woodcut: a town, seen over the brow of a hill, its trees and sleepy church making it look perhaps a little more like Bethlehem, Pennsylvania, than Bethlehem in Judea. Brooks had visited the Holy

Land shortly after Lincoln's death, and the peace he found there moved him deeply after the horror and bloodshed of the Civil War at home:

> I remember standing in the old church in Bethlehem, close to the spot where Jesus was born, when the whole church was ringing hour after hour with splendid hymns of praise to God, how again and again it seemed as if I could hear voices I knew well, telling each other of the wonderful night of the Savior's birth . . . for ever there will be a singing in my soul.[4]

Like his other lyrics, "O Little Town of Bethlehem" was meant for singing. Back home in Philadelphia, his church organist was a man who, as church organists often do, occupied his business in great commercial matters during the week, in this case real estate, only slipping on his organ shoes at the weekends. It seems that, on this occasion, Lewis Redner spent too much time on his business and not enough on his music. When Brooks asked him to set "O Little Town of Bethlehem" to music, he did what composers always do when handed a deadline: nothing. Then, months later, the tune came to him in a dream on Christmas Eve 1868. He hurriedly wrote it down next morning while shaving before church, and the children of his choir sang it for the very first time later in that Christmas season.

Redner's tune, "St. Louis," is the one often still sung today in the United States. English carol singers use a tune with a very different story to tell. Brooks published "O Little Town of Bethlehem" in 1891. In 1903, a decade after his death, it was included in *Christmas Songs and Easter Carols*. Around the same time, a raggle-taggle group of English eccentrics was tramping the lanes and villages of the British Isles, cycle-clips in hand, wax-disc-recording machine clutched bulkily under one arm, poking into pubs and church porches where old men and women sat puffing on pipes, thinking of the days before the railways came and remembering the songs they sang as the village lads marched away to see off Boney once and for all. Their visitors aimed to record this tradition before it was lost forever in the brave new world of the twentieth century. They were a mixed bunch: Percy Grainger, brilliant Australian of exotic personal tastes, in Lincolnshire; Marjorie Kennedy-Fraser, braving the winds of the Western Isles of Scotland; Cecil Sharp (who signed himself C#), in Somerset; and, working on the music of the counties around London, two friends who had met at the Royal College of Music in London and wrote to each other as "Dear V," "Dear RVW"—Gustav von Holst and Ralph Vaughan Williams.

Vaughan Williams loved English folk song. It touched something deep inside him. When he first heard the song he calls "Dives and Lazarus," he remarked: "Here's something I have known all my life, only I didn't know it."[5] The melodies and modes of these songs, and their habit of evolving organically between one village and the next, permeated both his and Holst's musical philosophy (Holst's "von" prudently dropped as German-sounding surnames became less socially desirable, a policy also adopted by the Royal family).

One sunny day in 1903, on one of his habitual field trips collecting songs, Vaughan Williams found himself in the leafy lanes of Forest Green, Surrey, scribbling furiously as a knobbly old villager, Mr. Garman, sang to him. As usual, other versions of the same song appear simultaneously elsewhere. Cecil Sharp collected this version in Hampshire at about the same time:

> I am a ploughboy stout and strong
> As ever drove a team;
> And three years hence asleep in bed
> I had a dreadful dream.
> And as the dream has done me good,
> I've got it put in rhyme:
> That other boys might read and sing
> My dream when they have time.
>
> Me thought I drove my master's team,
> With Dobbin, Ball and Star;
> Before a stiff and handy plough,

As all my master's are:
But found the ground was baked so hard,
And more like brick than clay;
I could not cut my furrow clean,
Nor would my beasts obey.

The ploughboy whips and lashes his oxen, until

The thunder roared from underground,
The earth it seemed to gape:
Blue flames broke forth, and in those flames
A dire gigantic shape.
"Soon shall I call thee mine," it cried,
With voice so dread and deep,
That quivering like an aspen leaf
I wakened from my sleep.

The mixture of a kind of didactic, sermonizing morality with an almost pagan, pre-Christian imagery is typical of this kind of folk song. This was music to keep your ploughboy honest as well as keep him entertained. The tune is sturdy and strong, good for marching up and down a muddy field. Nice and easy to sing too: four lines, all the same length; the music of lines one, two, and four exactly the same; a vocal range of an octave plus a note, the highest note touched just once in the third line; the melody nicely shaped, made mostly of scale patterns, with no awkward leaps. Easy to learn, and easy to remember. Perfect for a large group of not particularly expert musicians to sing and to enjoy singing. Vaughan Williams remembered these qualities when he undertook the job of musical editor of *The English Hymnal*, published in 1906.

Vaughan Williams liked giving congregations decent tunes, with proper harmony for choir and organ. He garnered good tunes for his book from anywhere he could find them: the psalters and hymns of early English Protestantism, Lutheran chorales, original melodies, and folk song. Not, however, the rather purple chromaticism of Redner's tune, distinctly American in flavor. Vaughan Williams preferred his choirs to sing the harmony of Bach and Tallis than indulge the "debased" tastes of Victorians like Barnby and Stainer. For "O Little Town of Bethlehem" he turned to the tune he had rechristened "Forest Green," after the village where he had first heard it sung by Mr. Garman.

It doesn't quite fit. Typically, Brooks varies his metrical scheme by inserting a seven-syllable line at line five. The tune has the more regular eight, six, eight, six, eight, six, eight, six shape known as "double common" meter. This slightly spoils the effect of Brooks's rather subtle hint of metrical variety. But Vaughan Williams knew what he was doing. The tune scrubs up beautifully, brought in from the fields and wearing its polite new Sunday suit with impeccable modesty and manners. If you didn't know, you might almost never guess what a rackety upbringing it had. A triumph of the veneer of Victorian rectitude.

There are plenty of other tunes to these words. Most are congregational. Some, like Joseph Barnby's "Bethlehem," were written for these words; others, like Uzziah C. Burnap's "Ephratah," were not. Walford Davies follows the German habit of adding a scriptural recitative before his charming melody, usually sung as a choir anthem rather than congregationally. At least one other folk tune, from Cornwall, has joined the shining throng. Needless to say, editors have found it necessary to fiddle around with Brooks's careful text. His line "Son of the Undefiled" in the (usually omitted) fourth verse has become "Son of the mother mild," which is a bit wet, and Edgar Pettman follows the practice of the first published version with music (but not Brooks's original published text) in reversing the order of the two halves of verse two, which is a bit odd (both work perfectly well). Like so many carols, this one is part of a tradition that is still evolving.

So next time these words and those notes work their familiar magic, remember the people who wove that magic for us: an American who imported peace from the Middle East; two dreamers—a naughty ploughboy and a real estate salesman; a devil in a puff of blue smoke; an English genius taking off his cycle-clips; and Mr. Garman of Forest Green, Surrey.

"O Little Town of Bethlehem"

O morning stars, together
Proclaim the holy birth!
And praises sing to God the King,
And peace to men on earth.
For Christ is born of Mary
And gathered all above,
While mortals sleep the Angels keep
Their watch of wondering love.

How silently, how silently,
The wondrous gift is given;
So God imparts to human hearts
The blessings of His Heaven.
No ear may hear His coming,
But in this world of sin,
Where meek souls will receive Him still,
The dear Christ enters in.

O holy Child of Bethlehem,
Descend to us, we pray!
Cast out our sin and enter in,
Be born in us to-day.
We hear the Christmas angels,
The great glad tidings tell;
O come to us, abide with us,
Our Lord Emmanuel!

December 25: Christmas Day

"Good Christian Men, Rejoice"

he collector Joshua Sylvester helpfully categorized traditional folk carols into six types. If we put all our folk carols together as one group, we can tentatively make a similar categorization of our carol repertoire as a whole, at least as far as musical origins are concerned. Such a list might look something like this: folk carols; pre-Reformation liturgical music, including plainsong; composed or "art" songs; Protestant hymns and psalms; tunes borrowed from instrumental and other repertoire; children's songs; secular "party" songs; and German chorales.

As with Sylvester's list, it's an inevitably leaky and porous system of classification, with plenty of crossover and subdivision. But a glance at the contents page of this book, or at the pieces in your favorite carol book or service of Nine Lessons, may perhaps suggest that it might help us to discern some sort of order among the tangled branches of our carol family and its ever-spreading and eternally-evolving diaspora.

German chorales are hymns. Just songs, really. They are terrific for congregational singing, because that's what they were designed for. Martin Luther was their principal, but not their only, begetter. Like Vaughan Williams and Sharp four hundred years later, he and his successors were perfectly happy to co-opt tunes from all over the place: folk songs, drinking songs, marching songs, lullabies, tunes by earlier composers, and even Catholic plainsong alongside their own original compositions. Anything, as long as it had a good tune.

Like the Catholic musical liturgy it replaced, the chorale repertoire has songs for each phase of the Christian year. This makes them a particularly useful resource at Christmas. The repertoire has given us familiar items at Advent (*"Wachet auf"* and "Sion Hears the Watchmen Calling"); Christmas (*"Quem pastores"* and "Jesus, Good Above All Other"); Epiphany (*"Wie schön leuchtet der Morgenstern"* and "How Brightly Shines the Morning Star"), and everywhere in between. As usual, we happily help ourselves to the riches of another culture whenever it suits us.

One song stands representative of this repertoire here. We know it today as "Good Christian Men, Rejoice." To its creators in the Germany of the Reformation and earlier it is *"In dulci jubilo."*

This cheerful little song begins life with a charming legend attached. Heinrich Seuse (Henry Suso in anglicized form) was a fourteenth-century German monk. His writings are shot through with the idea of service derived from an equal love of God and man, and he developed for himself the title *"Diener der Ewigen Weisheit"*—"servant" (or, in some translations, "servitor") "of the eternal wisdom." Like some of the earliest Christian mystics he was much given to mortification of the flesh, and, like them, he was rewarded with many visions of God, saints, and angels. An account of one appears in the (possibly autobiographical) *"Leben Seuses"* (or *"Vita"*), translated here by Father Thomas Knox in 1865:

Seuse in mid-vision: two near-contemporary images

There came to him a youth, who bore himself as if he were a heavenly musician sent to him by God; and with the youth there came many other noble youths, in manner and bearing like the first, save only that he seemed to have some pre-eminence above the rest, as if he were a prince-angel. Now this same angel came up to the Servitor right blithely, and said that God had sent them down to him, to bring him heavenly joys amid his sufferings; adding that he must cast off all his sorrows from his mind and bear them company, and that he must also dance with them in heavenly fashion. Then they drew the Servitor by the hand into the dance, and the youth began a joyous ditty about the infant Jesus, which runs thus: "In dulci jubilo," etc.[1]

There is, of course, no tangible link between this account and the first appearance of the tune itself, in a German manuscript dated around 1400. But by the glory days of the Lutheran hymnal in the middle of the next century, it is clearly a well-established favorite. The tune appears in a number of such collections, the earliest extant example dating from 1533. A 1545 publication adds a new verse, possibly by Luther himself. The words are macaronic, alternating phrases in Latin and German, with the charming feature that the poet maintains the rhyme scheme between languages:

In dulci jubilo
Nun singet und seid froh!

The writer even manages to switch languages in midsentence, keeping grammar and syntax intact and flowing seamlessly from one language to the other, thanks to the ingenious use of the linking word *in*, which works in both:

Unsers Herzens Wonne
Leit *in praesepio.*

Wordsmiths of the Reformation across Europe couldn't resist having a go in their own vernacular. A version appears in *"Piae Cantiones"* in 1582 with the words alternating macaronically between Latin and Swedish. Scotsman Robert Wedderburn included an English version in "Ane compendious buik of Godly and spirituall sangis Collectit out of sundrye partes of the Scripture, with sundrye vther ballatis changeit out of prophaine sangis in godly sangis, for auoyding of Harlotrie,"[2] which contains by him and his two brothers and was published in 1567 (though all three Wedderburns died during the 1550s):

> In dulci Jubilo,
> Now lat vs sing with myrth and Jo
> Our hartis consolatioun lyis in præsepio,
> And schynis as the Sone, Matris in gremio,
> Alpha es et O, Alpha es et O.

Wedderburn's text is better than many of the later English versions. It's interesting to note that some of the first and best religious poets in English were Scotsmen like the Wedderburns and their great predecessor, William Dunbar.

From these beginnings the tune retained its place at the very heart of Lutheran music-making. There are harmonizations and elaborations by, among many others, Johann Walter, Hieronymous, and Michael Praetorius and Dietrich Buxtehude. J. S. Bach, for whom the chorale was the hemoglobin in his musical and theological bloodstream, used it a number of times.

Like so many others, the next stage in this carol's history is its encounter with inquisitively minded English musicians in the nineteenth century.

Robert Lucas Pearsall is something of an exception from the usual well-educated insider who shepherded our carols through the Victorian era. Born in Bristol to a Quaker army family, he trained and worked as a barrister and had no formal musical or literary training. After his marriage and the birth of four children, the family emigrated to Germany where he separated from his wife, bought a ruined medieval castle in Switzerland, and spent the rest of his life fixing it up, living in rooms

N dulci iubilo, Nu siun-

ge wij io io/ Then all tingh för oß för-

mo ligger *in præsepi o,.* Och som Solen
skijner

skijner/ *matris in gremio:* Alpha es &

ω, Alpha es & ω.
O Iesu paruule för tigh är migh so we/
Tröst migh i mitt sinne *O puer optime,*
Lätt migh tin godheet finne *O princeps gloriæ,*
Trahe me post te, trahe me post te.

O Patris charitas, O Nati lenitas,
Wijwore plat förderffuadh *per nostra crimina,*
Nu haffuer hā oß förwärffuadh *cœlorū gaudia,*
Eya wore wij thär/ Eya wore wij thär.

Vbi sunt gaudia Ther siunger man/Eya/
Hwar Englanar siunga *noua cantica,*
Och sielanar springa *in regis curia,*
Eya wore wij thär/ Eya wore wij thär.

In dulci jubilo in Latin and Swedish, 1582, maintaining the bilingual rhyme scheme.

he built alongside it, and indulging his interest in the art and history of southern Germany and the Alps. When he died in 1856, he was buried in the castle's own chapel.

Perhaps because of this highly individualistic approach to life, his music has a definite stylistic signature of its own. His interest in Renaissance polyphony led to a real mastery of contrapuntal choral texture, particularly when writing in many parts. His madrigal "Lay a Garland" is a fine synthesis of the melodic world of eighteenth-century glee composers like Samuel Webbe with the techniques and preoccupations of the more melancholic madrigalists of Tudor England. Pearsall also wrote and translated some of his own texts, and his two sets of self-taught skills, musical and verbal, come together in his version of *"In dulci jubilo."*

It's a fine piece of work. His handling of the unusual texture of five solo and four choral vocal lines is masterly, and he wrings much expressive potential from his own version of the macaronic text and the stately triple-time dance rhythm of the melody.

Pearsall (the *da* before his surname was added later by his daughter in a reverse maneuver to that made by Holst some decades later) gave us the version often sung by choirs today.

There are others. A version in the hymnbook *Lyra Davidica* of 1708 gets rid of the Latin altogether. Another all-English rendering works from an early text that, in its turn, is entirely in German and begins, confusingly, *"Nun singet und seid froh,"* which is the second line of the original macaronic lyric. G. R. Woodward included his own translation (where he even managed to sneak in an extra Latin word, his little favorite *io*) in the *Cowley Carol Book.*

John Mason Neale and Thomas Helmore produced a version, though, most unusual for them, they misread their source. They were working from the version printed in *Piae cantiones*, given above. On the third system the Swedish word *ligger* has two syllables to the German and English one (*leit, lies*). Helmore read the two notes as "double-longs," wheras they are in fact "shorts" (in modern notation in 6/4 time, quavers instead of dotted minims. Neale gave the spurious long notes words:

"News! News!" in verse one. It's a bad mistake and completely ruins the flow of the melody.

Neale's text (often with the offending phrase omitted) is the one we know today: "Good Christian Men, Rejoice."

As usual, there is an almost infinite variety of versions, each subtly different, each seeking to translate something better or translate it back, or modernize the spelling, or unmodernize the grammar to make it more like the Latin or less like the Latin, or take out the word *men* or put it back in.

The tune has become the province of pop and folk bands as well as early music ensembles and choirs of all kinds. Mike Oldfield took it to number 4 in the UK charts in January 1976.

Quite right too. We're back with the dancing angels. Perhaps in some ways Oldfield and his ilk get closer to the hallucinatory spirit of Seuse's vision than surpliced choirboys do. Carols show off different bits of their genetic makeup as each generation discovers how to use them.

What this one brings to the modern choirstall and carol service is the faithful, earthy, determined love of singing that was the musical hallmark of the European Reformation and of one man above all other: Martin Luther.

"In dulci jubilo"

In dul - ci ju - bi - lo,___ Nun sin - get und sie froh!___

Un - sers Her - zens Won - ne Leit in prae - se - pi - o,___ Und

leuch - tet als die Son - ne Ma - tris in gre - mi - o,___

Al - pha es et O!___ Al - pha es et O!

O Jesu parvule   O Patris caritas!
Nach dir ist mir so weh!   O Nati lenitas!
Tröst mir mein Gemüte   Wir wären all verloren
O puer optime   Per nostra criminal
Durch alle deine Güte   So hat er uns erworben
O princeps gloriae.   Coelorum gaudia
Trahe me post te, Trahe me post te!   Eia, wären wir da, Eia, wären wir da!

Ubi sunt gaudia
Nirgend mehr denn da!
Da die Engel singen
Nova cantica,
Und die Schellen klingen
In regis curia.
Eia, wären wir da, Eia, wären wir da!

"O Come, All Ye Faithful"

("Adeste fideles")

f you asked a group of English carolers which item in their repertoire links Portugal, Benedictine monks, and the Jacobite rebellion of 1745, would they say "O Come, All Ye Faithful"? Probably not.

From the earliest days of the Reformation, English Catholics sought sanctuary in continental Europe. One of the less notable among these exiles of conscience was John Francis Wade, the devout and musical son of a cloth merchant based in Leeds, who found himself caught up in the strong tide of anti-Catholic sentiment in the decades following the "Glorious Revolution" of 1688. Wade fled to France in around 1731, aged about twenty. He found sanctuary first in Flanders and then at the Benedictine Abbey in Douai, not far from Paris, putting his liturgical knowledge and musical skills to good use as the monks' musical scribe and copyist.

Wade copied out the Latin hymn *"Adeste fideles"* several times during the 1740s and 1750s. He included it in his neat, careful collections of devotional music, all good Catholic stuff, alongside hymns to the Virgin and prayers for the king. The *"Adeste"* is a thing of great charm: four verses, a lilting melody in triple time, and a brief refrain, *"Venite adorate Dominum"* (changed after the first edition to *"Venite adoremus Dominum"*).

It soon proved popular. In 1781, it was published in England in *An Essay or Instruction for Learning the Church Plainchant*, probably edited by Samuel Webbe and others. Ten years later, Webbe made a more extended arrangement of the tune and published it as number six ("Christmas Day") of his *Motets for the Year*. Both versions, and all subsequent editions, contain a notable alteration from Wade's original. The tune is now in four beats in a bar rather than three. Perhaps it was Webbe's idea. Thanks to him, we approach Bethlehem at the march, not the minuet.

The 1781 *Essay* is a teaching manual, full of practical information about scales, intervals, and clefs (or "cliffs," as it calls them), and the pros and cons of the four-and five-line stave. It is striking how many of our carol tunes began life in musical textbooks of this kind.

The *Essay* is also explicitly Catholic in content. Webbe was an important figure in the tentative rebirth of Catholic music in England, necessarily limited to private chapels such as the one attached to the Portuguese Embassy in Lincoln's Inn Fields, where he was organist. This was the only place in London where the Catholic liturgy could be celebrated. In 1795, the Duke of Leeds attended a service there and heard *"Adeste fideles."* He liked it so much that he commissioned another arrangement from Thomas Greatorex, composer, astronomer, organist of Westminster Abbey and later confidant of Bonnie Prince Charlie, and added this version to the program for his 1797 season of "Concerts of Ancient Music."

From there, it found a ready place in musical soirées and society entertainments. The journal *Harmonicon* for March 10, 1824, included a review of a typically eclectic musical program of, among much else, oboe concerti (". . . Mr. Ling has been practising since last season . . ."), solo songs (". . . warbled by Miss Stephens, with her usual success . . ."), and this hymn (". . . we should like, by the by, to know the name of the composer of this beautiful hymn. It is called Portuguese, and if the author be a native of Portugal, he need not be ashamed of owning it . . .").

Many composers were suggested. The putative Portuguese link produced a parade of possibles, including the seventeenth-century "Musician King" John IV, his son, and Marcos Antonio da Fonseca, also known as "Portugal" (who was actually born twenty years after the first known source of the hymn). English candidates included Thomas Arne. Vincent Novello was said to have introduced it (Novello's daughter Mary Cowden Clarke said that he thought it was by the seventeenth-century English composer John Reading, which has no possible justification on stylistic or any other grounds). Handel was mentioned; the music does contain echoes of the triumphant, march-like style of other Handel-based hymns like "Thine Be the Glory" or "Joy to the World," but no suitable Handelian source comes to mind, and it seems highly unlikely that his music would have been sufficiently well-known in France to be parodied in this way.

Confusion reigned. By 1825 the French composer Charles François Angelet could publish variations on the tune and call his piece *"Air portugais de Handel, varié pour le piano forte,"* thus neatly combining two popular attributions, both wrong.

Nobody mentioned Wade, despite the fact that the several copies that made it to England from Douai were all signed by him. That connection wasn't spotted until the twentieth century. Nor was an intriguing musical coincidence.

In 1744, just as Wade was working on his manuscript copies of the hymn at the monastery in Douai, the Opéra-cômique up the road in Paris put on a brand-new piece, all preposterous plot and thwarted desire. Presumably the monks didn't queue up to buy tickets, but the opera featured a tune called *"Air Anglois"* that has remarkable similarities to the *"Adeste"* melody. The coincidence of date and geography is striking.

Like the tune, the words set off around Europe without an author's name attached. Editors and compilers attributed them to more or less anyone they could think of, often, for no apparent reason, the thirteenth-century Saint Bonaventure. Then, at around the turn of the nineteenth century, the French Abbé, Étienne Jean François Borderies, decided to add three new Latin verses to take in more of the gospel Christmas story. Another (eighth) verse was added a few decades later by an unknown writer to include the magi, taking the hymn right through the whole Christmas season and up to the Epiphany.

English hymn writers couldn't resist the temptation of translating. The first English version dates from around 1797. A hymnologist writing in the 1890s knew of nearly forty versions. A century later the number had risen to at least fifty. The one that stuck first appeared in print in 1852.

Francis Oakeley was incumbent at the Margaret Street Chapel,

Marylebone (later rechristened All Saints'), and a leading devotee of the Oxford Movement, following John Henry Newman to Rome and ending up as a canon of Westminster Cathedral. Rather conveniently for our purposes, Oakeley translated only the first four verses of *"Adeste fideles,"* the ones written by Wade. This is his first go at the opening:

O come, all ye faithful,
Joyfully triumphant

His many later versions add many small changes of detail.

The Latin of verses five to eight, by Borderies (and anon.), were subsequently translated into English by William Thomas Brooke, like Oakeley a convert, though this time into the Church of England (from the Baptists), rather than out of it. His four verses were published in 1885, inserted in the middle of Oakeley's to form a coherent chronological and scriptural narrative.

The hymn earned itself a place in the influential *English Hymnal* of 1906 (actually, two places: the four Wade/Oakeley verses appear on their own at number 28 in the Christmas section, the longer "Complete version," including the Borderies/Brooke verses, at number 614 as a processional). The musical arrangement is approaching its modern form, too, with the familiar rousing pile-up of the voice parts in the refrain.

We have the hymn we know today. What we don't have is any real idea about who wrote it, where it came from, or how it got here. The pot bubbles with theories.

The Portuguese association was around for a long time. There are various possible explanations. A modern Portuguese scholar states unambiguously that there were two copies of the *"hino de natal chamado Adeste Fidelis,"* ascribed to John IV of Portugal and dated 1640, in John's own library, lost in the Lisbon earthquake of 1750. Catherine of Braganza was John IV's daughter. When she married Charles II of England in 1662, she set up her own Catholic establishment, with music, in the Queen's Chapel in London. Samuel Pepys attended service there, and was much taken with both the music ("very good endeed") and the women ("my lady Castelmayne looks prettily in her nightclothes"), though not the liturgy ("frivolous").[1] Perhaps Catherine brought the *"Adeste"* with her, a sort of musical memento of home and Daddy.

David Baldwin, Serjeant of the Vestry at the Chapel Royal, notes that from 1667 Catherine's household included a group of eleven Portuguese "Franciscan Friars" (not Capucins, as Pepys wrongly identified them), who may themselves have imported or written the hymn. Baldwin thus evocatively invites us to "picture the origin and first rendition of the 'Adeste Fideles' amongst a group of friars each wearing a brown habit, hood and capuce with a seven decade rosary, a cord girdle, and sandals, singing in The Queen's Chapel."[2]

Or, perhaps the source of the Portuguese title is just a geographical coincidence. One of Wade's copies is known to have been made for the English College in Lisbon. Someone heard it there, found himself posted to the Embassy in London, and brought it with him. It's not the strangest itinerary in this book.

Alas, the most likely explanation is also the least romantic: the visit to the Embassy chapel one sunny Sunday morning in 1797 by the Duke of Leeds. Pity, really.

What is the original source of the music?

The alleged seventeenth-century origin can be safely discounted. It doesn't sound like anything else from the period, and certainly not like anything by John Reading, senior or junior, or John IV.

In 1910, the scholar and musical journalist G. E. P. Arkwright uncovered the "Air" from the opera of 1744, and noticed its similarity to the *"Adeste."* He suggested that both tunes might be variants of some forgotten original, perhaps an English folk song (hence "Air Anglois"). Thus, says Arkwright, "a really fine tune (the *"Adeste"*) was compounded out of rather incongruous materials . . . by some choirmaster (probably between *c.* 1740 and 1750), for the use of a Roman Catholic choir."[3] Uncannily, Arkwright has almost precisely described J. F. Wade without knowing of his existence. He has almost tripped over the truth while wandering in the historical shadows.

Others thought the "Air Anglois" might be a deliberate parody of the hymn, named in ironic honor of its author, the serious-minded Englishman scribbling away in his cloister. That's how ballad-opera works: give your audience a comic version of a song they already know in a more serious form, just as John Gay was doing in London.

Another writer noticed that French hymnbooks of the nineteenth century used the opening line for a number of hymns for different seasons of the church year, like this Easter hymn:

Adeste, fideles, laeti triumphantes,
Inane sepulcrum conspicite
(O come, all ye faithful, joyful and triumphant,
Come and behold the empty tomb)

Perhaps there is an element of a conventional formula here, part of a common library of verbal gestures, without a single identifiable author.

Then, in the 1940s, Dom John Stéphan of the Benedictine Abbey at Buckfast, in Devon, published "The Adeste Fideles: a study on its origin and development."[4] It's a first-rate piece of research. Stéphan had the happy knack of combining the most painstaking scholarship with a real enthusiasm for his subject and an engaging and readable style.

Stéphan identified six copies of the hymn from Wade's pen, the earliest (now lost) from around 1744 (later scholars have suggested a slightly earlier date). He dated his sources by comparing the versions of the words and careful examination of watermarks. The earliest book lacked a cover and, therefore, Wade's signature, but it is clear from comparisons with the other signed copies that it is from the same hand.

Stéphan looked carefully not just at the physical sources but also their context and provenance. He noticed that the earliest copy contains a prayer for the king, with music, immediately before the *"Adeste."* This is a conventional enough gesture, with one striking detail: this particular prayer is for "regem nostrum Jacobum: our King, James." Catholics never recognized the overthrow of James II. To them, he remained the lawful king of England. When he died in 1701, he was succeeded by his son James Francis Edward. This prayer is for James III.

The potential link between this "Jacobite" manuscript and revolutionary Catholicism in Britain intrigued Stéphan. He noted that several copies or records of performances turned up in Catholic enclaves within the British Isles, like Stonyhurst and St. Mary's Priory, Dublin. Perhaps Wade's book, hymn, royal prayer and all, is part of the whipping-up of pro-Catholic sentiment at home in the period immediately before the '45 rebellion.

Modern scholars have gone further. Some claim that the words of the hymn itself are a clandestine appeal to English Catholics to support Bonnie Prince Charlie's insurrection, in the sort of under-the-bedclothes code that William Byrd, another Catholic in internal exile, wove into his own music 150 years before and would have instantly recognized. *"Fideles"* (the "faithful") are Catholics. "Bethlehem" is the true church in captivity (equivalent to Byrd and Tallis's "Jerusalem"). *"Natum videte, regem angelorum"* is a pun: Christ was born King of the Angels, but Charles Edward Stuart was born King of the English—Come and behold Him, *"regem Anglorum."* Wade added the instruction *"ad usum chori Anglorum"* ("for the use of English choirs") to some of the surviving signed copies, not only confirming that these copies were intended for England but also, perhaps, inviting his readers to spot the pun. Not his joke, of course. Readers who knew their Bede, as Wade's surely did, would have recognized Pope Gregory's famous quip about the little blond English boys in the forum: *"non Angli, sed Angeli."* Wade, like Gregory, wants to get these *"Angli"* back on the side of the *"Angeli,"* the Roman church.

Ingenious. But if it is a coded invitation to rebellion, it was too subtle for the stolid Hanoverian brain. Nobody noticed. The hymn was happily accepted into Georgian society. The Catholic call-to-arms became a Protestant tub-thumper. And both sides produced plenty of propaganda without resorting to Latin puns. As for the proximity of the "royal prayer," Webbe's earliest English edition of the *"Adeste"* places it alongside exactly the same musical prayer for the king, with the name changed to "Georgium." The copy that Wade sent to Portugal has the name "Josephus." It's a conventional gesture, of no great significance.

Stéphan also concluded that Wade wrote both words and music, though there is, in truth, no real evidence that he did. He certainly wrote it down, and in 3/4 time, in every copy he made. Why did later copyists and arrangers change it to 4/4? Is it better like that?

Many writers think so. They like the rousing march-like character of the version we sing today. But the lilting rhythm of Wade's first, triple-time, version is surely far more interesting, and certainly more varied. There's a lovely little cross-rhythm at the last *"Venite, adorate."* It is fluid, graceful, and irresistibly French.

Which creates another possibility. The tune carries distinct echoes of the character of the French *"Noël,"* such a quintessentially eighteenth-century creature, and its cousin, the folk song. It has the sequential refrain that is a feature of many such tunes, including the two in this book. It is also a little bit similar in musical outline to the royal prayer that precedes it, which also has a sequential refrain. Are both tunes (and the operatic *"Air Anglois"*) loose variants of some forgotten French folk song? Is there the still just-discernible twang of a rustic accent in the melody, which Wade and Webbe have not quite succeeded in scrubbing away?

If so, how did it turn into a Christmas carol?

Nice Christmassy words being bolted on to a familiar folk song is nothing new. Plenty of *"Noëls"* were given prettified sacred texts by clerics during the eighteenth century, mostly in French, some in Latin, some in both. Something of the style of these texts can be caught in this extract from a lyric by the prolific French hymn writer Charles Coffin (who is still much sung in translation today), published in 1736:

Profunda noctis otia
Cœlestis abrumpit chorus;
Natumque festo carmine
Annuntiat terris Deum.

Specum sacratam pervigil
Dum turba pastorum subit,
Eamus, & castis pia
Cunis feramus oscula.

At quale nobis panditur
Intrantibus spectaculum!
Præsepe, fœnum, fasciæ,
Parens inops, infans puer.

(The heavenly choir shatters the darkness of night and
  announces the birth of God on earth in joyful song.
O come, let us go to where the crowd of shepherds gathers to
  keep watch around the holy cave, and bring our pure and
  pious devotions to his cradle.
See how this marvel is opened to us: the crib, the grass, the
  humble cloths, the mother mild, the baby boy.)

The words of *Adeste, fideles* have something in common with this style.
Even the underlay of the Latin words seems somehow French, much
less heavily stressed than English Latin would be (try singing *"Venite,
adorate"* as Wade wrote it). Perhaps the first four Latin verses, like the
last four, are by some long-lost frilly French Abbé with a frilly French
name, set to a smartened-up version of some *chanson de campagne*.

   We don't really know. Lots of stories still swirl around the possible
origins of this hymn. As Stéphan comments with a world-weary sigh,
"legends spread easily, though they die slowly."[5]

The *"Air Anglois,"* as copied by Arkwright, 1910

Whatever its origins or its politics, *"Adeste fideles"* gives us something important. With its Anglicized offspring "O Come, All Ye Faithful," it takes us on a stirring stride through the liturgical meaning of the various acts and scenes of the story of the nativity, ending rousingly on Christmas Day itself: "Yea, Lord, we greet thee." It reeks of theology. This one is a genuinely ecclesiastical item. A hymn. It belongs in the choir stalls, and always has, whether or not the choir stalls in question were French, English, Portuguese, Protestant, or Catholic.

Pages 91–95 of Wade's "Jacobite" ms (c. 1744 or 1740), now lost, as reproduced photographically by Stéphan in 1947, containing the "royal prayer" (in two-part harmony) and the "Adeste fideles" in 3/4 time (though Stéphan has not found it necessary to include the last line of the last refrain from page 96, presumably the same as all the other refrains).

"O Come, All Ye Faithful"

God of God, Light of Light,
Lo! he abhors not the Virgin's womb;
Very God, Begotten not created.
Refrain

Sing, choirs of angels, Sing in exultation;
Sing, all ye citizens of heaven above!
Glory to God, In the highest;
Refrain

Yea, Lord, we greet Thee, Born this happy morning;
Jesus, to Thee be glory given;
Word of the Father, Now in flesh appearing.
Refrain

"And There Were Shepherds, Abiding in the Fields"

"While Shepherds Watched"

review of all the tunes and musical settings of "While Shepherds Watched" would easily fill a book twice the length of this one.

It would be worth it. There are hundreds. The names alone conjure up the magic of place, people, and association that these tunes evoke: "Fern Bank," "Tom's Boy," "Old Foster," "Comfort," "Liverpool," "Leicester," "Lyngham," "Lloyd," "Hail! Chime On," "Morchard Bishop," "Zadoc," "St. Cloud," "Roadwater," "Martinstown," "Pentonville," "Ford," "Bampton," "Bolton," "Bedford," "Otford," "Cambridge New," "Canterbury," "Cabyn," "Carolina," "Adderley," "Greetland," "Christchurch" (or "St. Christchurch"), "Redruth." Some can only be partially identified: the "Old Beer" tune, an "old Ranter melody," a tune "sung by the carolers at Barton-St-David," another "from the Thomas Hardy family manuscript." One is called simply "Christmas."

Their musical styles, too, allow glimpses into all sorts of corners of English life and its communal musical voice. Some have the sonorous, three-part harmony, tune doubled at the octave by tenors, which grew directly out of the old medieval technique of improvising a harmony around a familiar tune (when ordinary parish singers largely didn't sing from books because they couldn't afford them, couldn't read them, and had anyway known these tunes since childhood). Some have fancy little instrumental "symphonies" and sturdy two-part fugues striding between melody and bass in the middle, in the West Gallery or Sacred Harp manner. Many are folk songs. Some are borrowed from other hymns. The "Shropshire Funeral Hymn" is in a minor key, with the rich, modal harmonies and expressive shifts of chord reminiscent of Tallis.

Some versions, typically for carols, use a variant of the words. One or two add a refrain, like the splendid "Sweet chiming bells," which instead of telling the shepherds to "Fear not," wants them to "cheer up, faithful shepherds, cheer up!"—much more the sort of thing a sturdy English angel would have said under the circumstances.

As well as lending itself to all sorts of musical swaddling, the text is ripe for schoolyard parody. English readers of a certain age will remember versions from their own childhood, usually involving socks and changing channels on the TV. No doubt there are many others. One elderly singer recorded in the early 1970s has:

While shepherds watched their peas and 'ops
All boiling in the pot,
A lone angel came fallin' down
And spoiled the jolly lot.

The key to this hymn's enduring popularity must lie in its universality and its simplicity. It's about ordinary people and ordinary things: sheep, fields, men sitting on the ground about to tuck into their sandwiches and finding themselves caught up in a rather surprising bit of the Christmas story. It's engaging, characterful, and full of joy. When we sing the Christmas story, the shepherds are us.

It tells its familiar tale in language that is simple and direct. There are no words longer than two syllables, and even those tend to be clear, expressive adjectives, adverbs, and nouns, coloring in the narrative in bright, primary colors: *mighty, meanly, troubled, glory*. Modernizers should take note: *humankind* might tick certain boxes, but *mankind* is shorter. (And it's what the man wrote.)

It's impossible, then, to attempt here anything approaching a comprehensive review of the history of this unassuming little gem. A closer look at just two of its many musical incarnations will pretty much tell the entire history of congregational singing in England.

The story begins in the very earliest days of the Reformation. Christopher Tye was a fine composer for the old Latin rite of the pre-Reformation Catholic Church. Unlike some of his contemporaries, he was also an enthusiastic Protestant. When Edward VI came to the throne in 1547, Tye embraced the opportunities for musical innovation presented by the devout, reformist boy-king. Edward wanted his words in English, and his music simple enough not to get in the way of the words. Tye responded with a metrical version of "The Actes of the Apostles," set to his own music, four parts, little repetition, no drawing-out of words for musical effect. The idea was that moralizing little devotional verses of this kind could be sung at home, by anybody, for entertainment and spiritual enlightenment, and they were enormously popular. Literary quality, unfortunately, did not always keep up with popularity. Tye was no Thomas Cranmer:

> Which sayd, ye men of Galilee
> Why gaze ye up in bayne:
> Thys Jesus thus, up take from us
> Shal thus come downe agayne.

Routley describes Tye's verses as "from the literary point of view pure *Stuffed Owl* from end to end."[1]

Notwithstanding his rather clunky versifying, for our purposes the interest of Tye's "Actes" lies in the *meane* (top) part of the second half of his setting of chapter VIII, which goes:

Try singing it from "And through the regions crept" (note that middle C is on the lowest line of the stave). Sound familiar?

The story now proceeds with the progress of popular psalm singing through the reign of Elizabeth I and beyond. Tye arranged his verses in common meter, that is, four-line stanzas in a pattern of eight, six, eight, six syllables. The vast majority of the vast number of versions of the psalms produced at this time used this same meter. Any psalm could be sung to any tune in the same metrical pattern. The practice of mixing and matching text and melody, such a creative and confusing a part of this history, was born. At the same time, bits of tunes could migrate from one setting to another, or sometimes two could be sung at once if their harmonies matched (or even if they didn't, quite). Congregations, and, no less importantly, families, could sing their favorite psalms to tunes they already knew and liked: "the one whose sense suits 'Mount Ephraim',"[2] as Thomas Hardy later put it, or the one that Dad knows the chords to on the theorbo, or the kids can manage on the household chest of viols.

The *Whole Booke of Psalmes*, begun in Edward's reign, went through many hundreds of printings in the following century-and-a-half, gathering well-known tunes like *"Ein feste burg"* as it went. Queen Elizabeth allowed "an hymn" (meaning a psalm) to be sung "before and after" (but not during) the actual service, but their content was strictly limited to the items in the *Whole Booke*: canticles, creed, Lord's Prayer, psalms, and one or two other suitable texts. But no Christmas carols. Certainly not. To the new breed of Puritan parson, our semi-pagan country cousins are still a thing for the churchyard, not the church.

The ongoing popularity of psalm singing presented considerable opportunities to the musical entrepreneur. Thomas East was a printer, and in 1592 he issued a psalter. As usual, he shuffled the pack of tunes and texts to meet his market, and included a number of tunes not seen before in print. One of them, by the curious process of cross-referencing and borrowings familiar to anyone who has dabbled in folk traditions, is based on Tye's meane part of forty years before, tune in the tenor, as was customary. East also continued the slightly eccentric habit of the English psalter-makers of naming their tunes after a favorite place, or some other reference entirely unconnected with its text. He called this one "Winchester" (later rechristened "Winchester Old" when someone decided to use the name "Winchester New" for the tune to the Advent hymn "On Jordan's Bank the Baptist's Cry").

In 1696, a new psalm book eventually arrived to supersede the old one. The new text, printed without tunes, was by Nicholas Brady and the Poet Laureate, Nahum Tate. Their book was quickly followed by a supplement, in which they allowed themselves one, just one, Christmas hymn, which they called "Song of the Angels at the Nativity of our Blessed Saviour." Like Tye before them, they adopted the time-honored practice of putting a suitable section of the biblical narrative into a nice, manageable metrical scheme, for easy, practical singing to a familiar tune, the parish clerk bellowing out each line for the congregation to repeat in a technique known as "lining-out" (a splendidly practical bit of communal music-making which has the added advantage of saving money on books). The poem, "Whilst Shepherds Watched Their Flocks by Night," is usually ascribed to Tate, and it was the only Christmas carol that could legally be sung in English churches for most of the rest of the eighteenth century, which is at least partly why it caught on quite as spectacularly as it did.

Another reason is Tate and Brady's instinctive genius for simplicity. Subsequent editors and arrangers have fiddled around with many carols. Not this one. It doesn't need it. Apart from their first word, which has perhaps permissibly elided from their *whilst* to the slightly less sibilant *while* over the years, this is the very first English carol that we still sing in the version in which its authors wrote it. Three hundred years and counting. Tate and Brady's cheery little message of goodwill really does look as if it might begin and never cease.

Through its roots in the psalm traditions of the sixteenth to the early eighteenth centuries, "While Shepherds Watched" really does tell, all by itself, the story of a particular strand of the history of congregational singing in England. By their master-stroke of setting their text in a simple, well-known meter, its authors allowed it to spread its wings through the later eighteenth and nineteenth centuries and on into the twentieth, forming local alliances with favorite tunes in virtually every village, church, nonconformist chapel, brass band, and fireside snug in England. The results are rich, varied, personal, and deeply moving. Just one will have to stand representative here.

Thomas Clark was a Canterbury cobbler. In 1805 he published *A Sett of Psalm & Hymn Tunes with Some Select Pieces and an Anthem*, including an irresistibly jolly melody in "common" meter (with the last two lines repeated), which he set to the hymn "Grace 'Tis a Charming Sound." By the usual process of singers cheerfully nicking a tune to sing to different words with the same meter, his melody soon found itself attached to Tate's lyric "While Shepherds Watched." In this incarnation it gained widespread use, including in Dorset and the West country, which it has steadfastly hung on to more or less ever since. Clark spent much of his long life making music in parish churches and Sunday schools around Canterbury, and his tune bears the name of a pretty little town on the A229 between Maidstone and Hastings, where, perhaps, he wrote it one shady afternoon under the flinty bulk of the old church, the scent of hops wafting gently across the Weald, or taught it one Sunday morning to the children of the parish, accompanied by their uncles and cousins on serpents, clarinets, and harmoniums. The tune, and the town, are called Cranbrook.

Oddly, this tune, with its roots in the hop-fields of Kent, has ended up as the unofficial national anthem of Yorkshire. Some fifty years after Clark wrote his melody, the members of Halifax parish church choir were on a day out to Ilkley moor. As singers do, they whiled away the journey by singing their own (not very religious) words to their favorite hymn tunes. The story goes that they improvised a lyric about a man who chose to woo his girlfriend out on the moor without taking the obvious precaution of wearing a hat, leading indirectly to their both being eaten by ducks. The song, in the local dialect, is "On Ilkla moor baht 'at," a curious example of a folk song appearing to evolve from a composed song rather than the other way round.

It's one detail in the history of one song. On its own, it barely even hints at the extent of the melodic peregrinations of this carol around England, a sort of musical Mr. Pickwick, picking up friends as it goes. It met its long-term partner, the tune "Winchester," probably in the nineteenth century. In America it hooked up with an arrangement of an operatic number by Handel.

But the full richness and variety of its history will, like the shepherds, have to wait.

"While Shepherds Watched"

"Cranbrook"

"Winchester Old"

Whilst shep-herds watched their flocks by night, All sea-ted on the ground, The an-gel of the Lord came down, And glo-ry shone a-round.

"Fear not!" said he, for mighty dread
Had seized their troubled mind;
"Glad tidings of great joy I bring
To you and all mankind.

"To you, in David's town, this day
Is born of David's line
The Saviour, who is Christ the Lord,
And this shall be the sign:

"The heav'nly Babe you there shall find
To human view displayed,
All meanly wrapped in swathing bands,
And in a manger laid."

Thus spake the seraph and forthwith
Appeared a shining throng
Of angels praising God, and thus
Address their joyful song:

"All glory be to God on high,
And to the Earth be peace;
Good will henceforth from heav'n to men
Begin and never cease!"

"O Holy Night"

any different traditions hover over our carol repertoire like the stars on Christmas Eve.

This one is French, rooted in the music of the nineteenth-century Catholic Church, half-opera, half-soirée, designed to echo cavernously round the gloomy spaces of some vast Gothic church, reverently bellowed by a trained opera singer, all vibrato and shirt frills, accompanied by the kind of organ that can make the floor rattle.

The words came first. Placide Cappeau was born in Roquemaure, near Avignon, in 1808. At the age of eight he lost his right hand in an accident when he and a friend, a lad by the name of Brignon, had the bright idea of playing with a gun that Brignon's dad had rather thoughtlessly left lying about. By way of recompense Brignon *père* paid Cappeau's way through school. Despite his disability, young Placide did well, gaining among other accolades a prize for drawing (left-handed, presumably). He then went into the family business, making and trading in wine. Throughout, he wrote poetry, including some lyrics in the local Provençal language and a Byronic epic, which ran to nine thousand verses, about his hometown.

Like some other authored carols of the nineteenth century, this one seems to have been thrown together in something of a rush. The story goes that in 1847 the *curé* of Roquemaure, abbé Eugène Nicolas, asked his poet friend and parishioner to come up with something for a Christmas pageant he was organizing to raise money for the church window fund. Cappeau agreed, and promptly headed off on a business trip to Paris. On December 3, inspiration caught up with him on the road, and he wrote the poem there and then, in the carriage, halfway between Mâcon and Dijon.

Arrived in Paris, Cappeau and his poem found themselves in the company of the leading opera composer Adolphe Adam through an introduction from the soprano Emily Laurey. Laurey had sung in Adam's 1840 opéra-comique "La Rose de Péronne." Cappeau knew Laurey's husband, Pierre, a civil engineer who was building the new suspension bridge in Roquemaure. Adam set the poem to music in just a few days, and Emily gave the first performance at midnight Mass back in Roquemaure on Christmas Eve 1847.

The song, known initially as the "Noël d'Adam," was a big hit, though its composer lived to witness only the beginning of its world-wide popularity. Adolphe Adam died in 1856 at the age of fifty-two, universally feted for his many operas, perfectly tuned to the insatiable Parisian appetite for melody, melodrama, and magic.

Far from uniquely in this book, the song's popularity caused its author a problem. This wasn't the usual problem, though. Normally, editors and performers start changing and fiddling about with the words and the original author tries to stop them. In this case, Cappeau tried to distance himself from some aspects of his original lyric, but failed.

Cappeau was a man of his times. Born out of the turmoil of post-Revolutionary France, he was part of the generation that inherited the intellectual currents of the Enlightenment. He was a socialist, a free thinker, and an anticlerical. In time, with the stern eye of the abbé Eugène no longer upon him, he came to regret some of the more orthodox doctrinal aspects of his poem and tried to alter them.

Here is the opening of Cappeau's poem as he wrote it in 1847:

Minuit, chrétiens, c'est l'heure solennelle
Où l'Homme-Dieu descendit jusqu'à nous,
Pour effacer la tache originelle,
Et de son Père arrêter le courroux.
(Christians, it is midnight: the solemn hour when the God-Man

came down to us to wipe away original sin and end his father's anger.)

Nearly thirty years later, in 1876, a character in Cappeau's epic poem (a lover called, perhaps coincidentally, Placidie) is seated one day at the organ accompanying himself in the *"Cantique à l'orgue de Roquemaure."* This is the opening:

Minuit, chrétiens, c'est l'heure solennelle,
Où dans l'heureux Bethléem, vint au jour
Le messager de la bonne nouvelle
Qui fit, des lois de sang, la loi d'amour.
(Christians, it is midnight: the solemn hour when to joyful Beth-
lehem came in the daylight the messenger of good news who
turned the laws of blood into the law of love.)

The expectant Christians still await the solemn midnight hour, but the God-Man and original sin are gone, replaced by a messenger of good news who comes to replace the law of blood with the law of love. It's an important instance of the kind of doctrinally liberal, socially aware take on the person and teachings of Jesus that begins to echo through the century into the lives and work of writers like Louisa May Alcott, Robert Tressell, and beyond.

It also provides a link to the translator of Cappeau's poem.

It's interesting that certain political and intellectual currents keep recurring in this book. Several of our carol writers were visceral oppo-nents of slavery, men like James Montgomery in England, Phillips Brooks and James Lord Pierpont in the United States, and Cappeau in France. Among American carol writers, the Unitarian church exercises a disproportionate influence, too, taking in pieces as diverse as this one and "Jingle Bells."

John Sullivan Dwight was a Unitarian minister (at least to begin with).

Perhaps there is something in the Unitarian worldview that lends itself to carol writing. By rejecting the doctrine of the Trinity, Unitarians bring the figure of Jesus and the events of his life into a sharper and more human focus. The story of the nativity, of a human child, certainly seems to hold a special appeal for the movement's versifiers and hymn writers.

Dwight trained for the Unitarian ministry at the heart of the New England establishment, Harvard Divinity School, but was soon swept along in the more exotic waters of transcendentalism. Transcendentalism favored hard work, communal living, and a liberal approach to Christian teachings, and counted writers and thinkers like Emerson, Thoreau, Hawthorne, and Alcott among its adherents (with varying degrees of adhesiveness). Dwight joined the transcendentalist community at Brook Farm, near Boston, as a music teacher. Brook Farm was an experiment, in some respects not unlike the ones attempted by the Chartists and Robert Owen in the United Kingdom, and by other groups of like-minded idealists across the United States. Like so many of these attempts at communal living and doctrine-free religion, it faltered on the familiar stumbling blocks of practicalities, human nature, and money. Some of its members yearned for the old religious certainties. One member commented fearfully, "I suspected rosaries rattling under aprons"[1] and was proved horribly right when several of his fellow residents, including the founder's wife, came out as Catholics. Others chafed under the harsh realities of collective living, which in practice turned out to mean collective poverty. Novelist Nathaniel Hawthorne was a founding member, though he didn't stay long, describing the atmosphere as "thraldom and weariness" and later satirizing the community in his novel *A Blithedale Romance*.

Dwight found his escape in music. Following the collapse of the Brook Farm experiment in 1847, he founded *Dwight's Journal of Music*, earning a reputation as one of the country's leading music critics and a passionate advocate of the music of Beethoven.

In 1855 Dwight rendered Cappeau's "Noël" into English.

Several threads of his intellectual hinterland flutter behind the angel-wings of Dwight's translation: his powerful musicality; the conflicted piety of the lapsed minister who has lost his vocation but assuredly not his faith; a horror of slavery; and the inclusivity of his youthful idealism.

In some ways Dwight continues the process of detoxing the doctrinal content of the poem that Cappeau himself began with his second, later version. This movement from religious orthodoxy to contemporary social comment can be seen within the course of the poem itself too.

It is important to note that Dwight's version is not a literal translation. Partly this is because, as an able musician, Dwight knew that singability is always far more important than trying to shoehorn the exact shade of meaning of every last *circonflexe* into the English. Partly, also, it is an attempt to reflect his own worldview in his words. All three versions are given below, verse by verse: Cappeau's original French; a reasonably literal prose translation; and Dwight's singing version.

Comparing them may be instructive.

1. *Minuit, chrétiens, c'est l'heure solennelle*
Où l'Homme-Dieu descendit jusqu'à nous,
Pour effacer la tache originelle,
Et de son Père arrêter le courroux.
Le monde entier tressaille d'espérance,
À cette nuit qui lui donne un Sauveur.
Peuple, à genoux, attends ta deliverance
Noël! Noël! Voici le Rédempteur!
(CAPPEAU)

(Christians, it is midnight: the solemn hour when the God-Man
came down to us to wipe away original sin and end his father's
anger. The whole world trembles with hope on this night that
gives us a savior. People, to your knees! Await your deliverance!
Noel, noel! Behold, the Redeemer!)

O holy night, the stars are brightly shining,
It is the night of the dear Saviour's birth;
Long lay the world in sin and error pining,
'Till he appeared and the soul felt its worth.
A thrill of hope the weary world rejoices,
For yonder breaks a new and glorious morn;
Fall on your knees, Oh hear the angel voices!
O night divine! O night when Christ was born.
O night, O holy night, O night divine.
(Dwight)

(Right from the start of the poem, Dwight does away not just with
  original sin and the *"Homme-Dieu"* but also with the Father's
  wrath and, with it, the need for deliverance by the Redeemer.
  His *"chrétiens"* are far less passive observers of their own fallen
  state than Cappeau's.)

De notre foi que la lumière ardente
Nous guide tous au berceau de l'Enfant,
Comme autrefois une étoile brillante
Y conduisit les chefs de l'Orient.
Le Roi des rois naît dans une humble crèche;
Puissants du jour, fiers de votre grandeur,
À votre orgueil, c'est de là que Dieu prêche.
Courbez vos fronts devant le Rédempteur!
(Cappeau)

(The ardent light of our faith guides us all to the infant's cradle,
  as in other times a brilliant star led the kings of the East there.
  The King of kings is born in a humble stable; you, the mighty of
  your day, so proud of your grandeur, it is to your pride that God
  preaches. Bow down before the Redeemer!)

Led by the light of Faith serenely beaming;
With glowing hearts by his cradle we stand:
So, led by light of a star sweetly gleaming,
Here come the wise men from Orient land,
The King of Kings lay thus in lowly manger,
In all our trials born to be our friend;
He knows our need, To our weakness no stranger!
Behold your King! Before Him lowly bend!
(DWIGHT)

(The second verse takes us on the conventional narrative trajectory,
broadening out the story to take in the Epiphany, the bringing of
the good news to the *"chefs de l'Orient,"* the wise men, or magi.
Cappeau, perhaps unsurprisingly given recent events in France,
seems rather more keen than Dwight to put down the mighty
from their seat. Perhaps it was this passage, as much as his
stately march tune, that led Adam himself to refer to this song
as the *"Marseillaise réligieuse."* Politics hovered early over this
particular nativity.)

Le Rédempteur a brisé toute entrave,
La Terre est libre et le Ciel est ouvert.
Il voit un frère où n'était qu'un esclave,
L'amour unit ceux qu'enchaînait le fer.
Qui lui dira notre reconnaissance?
C'est pour nous tous qu'il naît, qu'il souffre et meurt.
Peuple, debout! Chante ta délivrance.
Noël! Noël! Chantons le Rédempteur!
(CAPPEAU)

(The redeemer has shattered every shackle. Earth is free, heaven
open. He sees a brother where once was a slave, and love unites
those whom iron once held in chains. Who will tell him that we
know him? It is for us all that he was born, suffered, and died.

People, arise! Sing of your deliverance. Noel, noel! Let us sing
about the redeemer!)

Truly He taught us to love one another;
His law is Love and His gospel is Peace;
Chains shall he break, for the slave is our brother,
And in his name all oppression shall cease,
Sweet hymns of joy in grateful Chorus raise we;
Let all within us praise his Holy name!
Christ is the Lord, then ever! ever praise we!
His pow'r and glory, evermore proclaim!
(DWIGHT)

Verse three completes the journey from first-century Palestine to nineteenth-century post-Revolutionary France and America. Here is the
explicit invitation to cast off the chains of your brother, the slave, in the
kind of imagery that echoes through the century. Cappeau, writing in
1847, on the very eve of the "year of revolutions," knew exactly what he
was evoking here. We are, in more ways than one, halfway between
Rousseau and Marx. *Peuple, debout!*

(This passage has, incidentally, caused some avoidable confusion
to translators who thought that *fer* (*iron*) was the object of the verb
enchaînait (*enchained*), and that the phrase *"L'amour unit ceux qu'enchaînait
le fer"* therefore means something like "love unites those who restrain
the sword," as one version has it. It doesn't. It means "love unites those
whom the iron held in chains." Dwight's readers in the New England
of the late 1850s could hardly have failed to catch the clinking, rattling
echoes of that particular choice of imagery.)

The later history of this song is testament to its popularity, with
several good stories attaching themselves along the way, at least some
of which are true.

It appeared in print in France, England, and America from about
1860. Most English publications use Dwight's words, though, as its popularity spread, others tried their hand. As for the music, interestingly, the

"ossia," inviting the singer to chuck in a few high notes at the end of the third chorus, is there from the beginning. In fact, the earliest surviving US publication, from 1871, gives two entirely discrete versions of the voice part, one presenting the tune straight, the other adding embellishments not just above but also below the original melody, giving the singer a range of a full two octaves. Both versions are given below.

A much-repeated story says that on Christmas Eve 1870 a French soldier emerged from his trench on the Franco-Prussian front line and began singing the *"Cantique de Noël."* Moved, the Prussians, instead of firing, replied with their own *"Von Himmel Hoch."* More carols followed. Alas, the story can't be verified, and may be a back-formation from the famous "Christmas truce" of 1914.

On Christmas Eve 1906 the song became the first piece of music to be broadcast live on the radio. Canadian engineer Reginald Fessenden set up the first ever AM broadcast at his base on Brant Rock, Massachusetts. His wife, Helen, takes up the story: "Three days in advance Reg had his operators notify the ships of the U.S. Navy and of the United Fruit Co. that were equipped with the Fessenden apparatus that it was the intention of the Brant Rock Station to broadcast speech, music and singing."[2] Reg introduced the program, then played some Handel on an Ediphone phonograph, then performed "O Holy Night" (which he ascribes, erroneously but understandably, to Gounod) himself, on the violin, and sang along in the last verse, though, as Reg comments with rueful modesty, "the singing of course was not very good." They ended with a Bible text, a "Merry Christmas" and a promise to broadcast again on New Year's Eve, which they did. The broadcast was received as far south as Norfolk, Virginia, and even the West Indies.

This song fills a particular niche in our carol repertoire. Among all the folk songs, psalm tunes, nursery rhymes, and hymns, this one is an art song. It is meant for a soloist, preferably one as plump and confident as the Christmas turkey. It doesn't really work sung by a choir, and certainly not by a congregation.

But, treated sympathetically, it can add something special to our

Christmas music making. It makes a splendid crescendo as the hush of that first holy night is thoroughly *brisé* by the shouts of *Noël!,* as it no doubt was by the angels, that first holy night.

Above all, it's a great tune.

"O Holy Night"

night_____ di vine!_____ O night, O night di

vine!

a tempo

Led by the light of Faith serenely beaming;
With glowing hearts by his cradle we stand:
So, led by light of a star sweetly gleaming,
Here come the wise men from Orient land,
The King of Kings lay thus in lowly manger,
In all our trials born to be our friend;
He knows our need, To our weakness no stranger!
Behold your King! Before Him lowly bend!
Behold your King! your King! before him bend!

Truly He taught us to love one another;
His law is Love and His gospel is Peace;
Chains shall he break, for the slave is our brother,
And in his name all oppression shall cease,
Sweet hymns of joy in grateful Chorus raise we;
Let all within us praise his Holy name!
Christ is the Lord, then ever! ever praise we!
His pow'r and glory, evermore proclaim!
His pow'r and glory, evermore proclaim!

"Lo, the Angel of the Lord Came upon Them"

· 10 ·

"Ding dong! Merrily on High"

n 1589 a manual of courtly dance was published by the
Frenchman Thoinot Arbeau. That isn't his real name. He was
actually a priest named Jehan Tabourot. "Thoinot Arbeau"
is a pen name and an anagram of his real name (though the anagram
doesn't quite work in modern spelling: you have to read *i* and *j* as the
same letter, Latin-style).

His book is called *Orchésographie*. Like so many of the productions
of the new commercial presses across Europe, it is a thing of beauty,
lavishly illustrated, carefully typeset on the page, with a gorgeous title
page, florid dedication, and handsome initial letters draped in foliage
and classical deities. His course of instruction in how to *"apprendre
a danser"* and *"battre le Tambour"* is set out in the form of a dialogue
between teacher and student, the approved method derived from
Socrates and much used at the time, for example by Thomas Morley
and our Scots friend John Forbes in their textbooks of music theory. The
teacher is the pseudonymous author Arbeau, the pupil a young man
called Capriol.

It's a charming and extremely interesting book. It tells you how to
tie and carry a large drum (and a sword), and what different national
styles of drumming are like, and gives extensive and detailed information about all sorts of dances, complete with woodcuts of a rather
self-conscious young couple in full fig doing the *"sault majeur"* and the
"pieds en l'air."

There is a great deal of music, painstakingly set up in movable type,
beautifully clear. There are drum rhythms, plenty of tunes for fife and

flute, and a gorgeous little love song for voices in four parts. Above all, there are "airs" (dance tunes).

Arbeau classifies these according to the type of dance: the *courante*, the *basse-dance*, the *gaillarde*. Within these classifications, many of the tunes have names: "*Air de la gaillarde appellee Anthoinette*," "*Branle de Poictou*." Some of the names imply a foreign origin: the "*Pavane d'Espagne*" and the "*Air de la gaillarde appelle La traditore my fa morire*."

Peter Warlock made memorable use of these melodies in his "Capriol Suite" for strings. Stravinsky drew on these resources, too, in his ballet *Agon*, with somewhat spikier results. They're folk tunes. The publication brings together a wealth of tunes bursting with what Cecil Sharp would have recognized as the "unconscious art" of the folk musician, very like its almost exact contemporary *Piae Cantiones*. It's wonderful stuff. There are many more riches waiting to be mined here.

Toward the end of the book Arbeau sets out his detailed dance steps alongside the melodies that go with them. This gives him an interesting problem: how to present the dance steps, which need to be read top-to-bottom, in proper alignment with the matching notes and beats of the music, which is read left-to-right. He comes up with an ingenious solution: put the musical stave vertically down the side of the page with the steps alongside:

Brilliant.

Among his last dances are a set of the type known as the *branle* (the *branle d'Escosse*, the *branle des Pois*, the *branle couppé nõmé Cassandre*), each with its own detailed directions for dancing—as explained in an exchange between our young pupil and a by now apparently rather exasperated teacher:

> **Capriol**: *Comment danciez vous ces branles que vous dictes?*
> **Arbeau**: *Vous le verrez par leur tabulature.*

Right at the end is a florid little melody, stretching vertically over two pages, with the grand-sounding name *"Branle de l'Official."*

The story now moves on three hundred years and four hundred miles north, into familiar *curriculum vitae* territory for the English carol. A folk tune of indeterminate origin, nothing whatever to do with Christmas, is discovered in an old book by an English clergyman, who adds words in a suitably old-fashioned style, publishes it in a carol book, and thus places it smack in the middle of our Christmas carol repertoire as if it had been there all its life, where it has stayed ever since.

George Ratcliffe Woodward belongs firmly in the tradition of idealistic, high church Anglican priests, scholars, and hymn writers who feature so strongly in this story. He served his ministry at St Barnabas', Pimlico, and at Little Walsingham in Norfolk, where he would sometimes play the euphonium in procession through the ruined abbey gateway and along the muddy edges of the turnip fields to the shrine (the Anglican one, of course). Like Baring-Gould, he wrote voluminously about saints and legends, and published books of poems. Like the earlier great partnership of Helmore and Neale he was fascinated by plainsong, Renaissance music, and the traditions of orthodox Christianity. Like them, too, he was part of a creative double act with a long-term musical collaborator, his Cambridge friend and fellow Caian, Charles Wood. Between them, their many books of Christmas music represent, alongside Sharp, the most important contributions to the repertoire between Helmore and Neale and the later work of Vaughan Williams, Percy Dearmer, and Martin Shaw.

"Ding dong! Merrily on High" first appeared in the *Cambridge Carol-Book* in 1924. The words are by Woodward, the tune is Arbeau's *"Branle de l'Official,"* harmonized by Wood with all his fastidious professorial craftsmanship.

Woodward's text has all the hallmarks of the received carol writer's style. There is the inverted syntax ("in heav'n the bells are ringing"); the archaic vocabulary (*e'en so, verily, riv'n*—Woodward originally wrote "the sky is *rent* with angels' singing," which was perhaps a bit obscure, and possibly a bit violent, even for his choristers and congregations); verb forms borrowed from Old English (*sungen* and *swungen*). Above all there is the fondness for dropping in a Latin refrain, in direct imitation of the macaronic carols of the fifteenth century: *"Gloria, Hosanna in excelsis."* This creates a seemingly endless melisma (where a single syllable is sung to an extended musical phrase). Other carols with roots in French popular song have this feature, too, and it gives them a very distinctive character. It works. No doubt the harmonious marriage of tune and words derives much of its appeal from the influence of one of Woodward's hobbies, bell ringing (if not from his other, beekeeping).

The words are, in truth, a bit odd. It's one of the curiosities of this history that some of the wilder flights of Victorian versifying have had much scorn heaped down on their heads, while others, including this one, have apparently passed the test of public acceptability without comment. It doesn't always seem logical. But, of course, liking something doesn't need logic. Woodward's words swing along very happily, the syllables matched gratefully to the chattering rhythm of the verses between the fluid *legato* refrain. It's short, and a welcome chance for the choir to sing something fast. Perhaps all this matters just as much as the words actually meaning anything.

One of the interesting things about scraping away at the history of the music is the chance to experience these tunes as they were before they became the carols we know today. Often, this means singing them to completely different words. In this case, it means getting up out of your chair and dancing the branle. Try it: Arbeau gives us the clearest possible lesson in how to do it, a sort of sixteenth-century exercise video.

> *Pied gaulche largy* means "put your left foot out."
> *Petit sault* is a "little jump."
> *Pied droit approché* is "bring your right foot in."
> *Pieds ioincts* is "feet together."
> Then you make a *double a droict* (do the same four steps to the right).
> Then when you're happy with that you can *empoigner la femme par le saulx du corps* (grab the lady round the waist), *l'eslevant en l'air pour la faire saulter* (pick her up as if she's jumping), then . . .
> . . . and . . . *pause.*
> *Très bien.*

It might not go in your carol service, but it should be fun at the party afterward.

Alors, encore une fois: Un, deux, trois . . .

"Ding dong! Merrily on High"

Ding dong! mer-ri-ly on high in heav'n the bells are ring - ing:
Ding dong! ver-i-ly the sky is riv'n with An - gel sing - ing.

Glo - - - - - ri - a, Ho - san - na in ex - cel - sis!

E'en so here below, below
Let steeple bells be swungen
And *i-o, i-o, i-o*
By priest and people be sungen
Refrain

Pray ye dutifully prime
Your matin chime, ye ringers
May ye beautifully rime
Your evetime song, ye singers
Refrain

· 11 ·

"Angels from the Realms of Glory"

he life story of our next carol contains familiar elements with a personal twist: traditional tune from France combined with words by a Scottish Moravian newspaper editor, one-time prisoner, and French Revolution enthusiast based in Sheffield.

At least in this case the tune possibly had some association with Christmas to start with. *Noëls* are tunes, once played by piping shepherd boys on the mountainsides of Provence and the Pyrenees. In the eighteenth century, published collections of Christmas Noëls were issued. Often, these volumes are the earliest source. There is, however, nothing to suggest that they were newly composed at the time of publication, so it is reasonable to infer that they have their origins in folk music, as their style strongly suggests. Many of them have the triple-time rhythm and rustic, dancelike qualities that Baroque composers used as a convenient shorthand for the bucolic (think of *Messiah,* and concertos by Corelli and Vivaldi). French composers liked to base florid little organ pieces on them, and there are many examples by Daquin and others.

Noëls were also sung in church. Sometimes they were incorporated into liturgical settings, with the words of the Mass or other proper text added to them. The best example is the *"Messe de Minuit"* by Marc-Antoine Charpentier, where a number of these tunes process cheerfully through the Mass, sometimes as instrumental interludes with the names of the tunes attached (*"Joseph est bien marié," "Ou s'en vont ces gais bergers,""A minuit fut fait un réveil"*) at other times as the musical basis for arty little treble solos (*dessus*) and learned fugues. The tunes scrub up very prettily, brought in from the fields to add a little rustic charm to Christmas festivities at the Bourbon court and the gilded churches of Parisian society, the musical equivalent of Marie-Antoinette's shampooed sheep down the hill at the Petit Trianon.

Another way of turning these tunes into sacred music was for the eighteenth-century publishers to give them brand-new words. Often these are evocations of suitable biblical scenes: shepherds dancing, babies sleeping, angels singing. Sometimes they take the form of mini-plays with named characters taking part in a narrative dialogue. The words were probably written by priests and have none of the dark, atavistic mystery of real folk carols from the Celtic fringes of Europe, with their strange, pagan imagery of ravens and holly, of life and death.

"Les anges dans nos campagnes" doesn't exist in any surviving printed source before the 1840s, but references and stylistic evidence strongly suggest origins in the eighteenth-century Noël repertoire. The words we sing to its melody today also appeared in print in the first half of the nineteenth century.

James Montgomery had one of the more rackety among many dodgy careers in this book. He was born in Ayrshire in 1771, the son of Moravian missionaries who sent him to a boarding school in Leeds while they sailed off to spread the gospel in the West Indies, where both soon died. The Moravian school in Leeds didn't allow the study of secular subjects, but young James developed an abiding interest in epic poetry. Perhaps unsurprisingly, under the circumstances, his school career was a failure, and he was sent as apprentice to a baker in Yorkshire. He continued to write poetry in the popular romantic manner, and had some success, though an attempt to forge a literary career in London failed, leading him to return north.

He became a journalist, for which his literary instincts were singularly unsuited, working on a paper called the *Sheffield Register*. Unusually, the *Register* took a strongly reformist line on libertarian issues such as the abolition of slavery and proper regulation of boxing, and in 1794 its editor, Joseph Gales, fled to Europe after troops arrived to arrest him for his public support of nascent revolutionary movements across the channel. Montgomery became editor in his stead, changing the name to the slightly more poetic *Sheffield Iris*. He maintained the paper's reforming zeal, and was twice imprisoned for libel, once for publishing a poem celebrating the storming of the Bastille (which may actually have been printed by his predecessor, not by him). Throughout, he wrote poetry. His themes exemplify the best and the worst of a particular kind of high-minded, free-thinking, early nineteenth-century dissenting Christianity. His opposition to slavery is resolute:

> Let tyrants scorn, while tyrants dare,
> The shrieks and writhings of despair;
> An end will come—it will not wait,
> Bonds, yokes, and scourges have their date,
> Slavery itself must pass away,
> And be a tale of yesterday.

Then there is a disturbing poem titled "An Indian Mother About to Destroy her Child," showing her "brooding o'er her sex's wrongs" before a graphic description of the crime, a white lotus-leaf wrapped round the baby's mouth to "still its cries." Another poem has an Englishwoman gazing at a painting of "an Aged Negro-Woman" and asking:

> Art thou a woman? . . .
> Look on thyself, thy kindred, home, and country,
> Then fall upon thy knees, and cry "Thank GOD,
> An English woman cannot be a SLAVE!"

Montgomery's best poems are his hymns. In 1825, ownership of the paper passed to a rival, and Montgomery devoted the rest of his life to hymn writing. He was very good at it. Of his four hundred or so hymns, a full one hundred found a regular place in the repertoire. Several have it still. As with all the best devotional lyricists, part of Montgomery's trick is a profound and easy familiarity with the rich heritage of English liturgical writing, particularly the psalms.

In 1817, a new vicar, the Reverend James Cotterill, arrived at

Sheffield's main parish church. Some years before, Cotterill had published *A Selection of Psalms and Hymns Adapted to the Services of the Church of England*, but found his new parishioners unwilling to use his carefully crafted versions. In an inspired move, he turned for help to his local newspaper editor, James Montgomery. Metrical versions of psalms, specifically aimed at the practical needs of ordinary worshippers, had been the backbone of congregational singing in England since the Reformation, and they were hugely popular. Montgomery was taking his place in a noble tradition. Their key features are a regular meter (allowing them to be sung to any suitable tune that the congregation already knows), striking imagery, and directness of language. To a born-and-bred nonconformist like Montgomery, this was mother's milk. His version of Cotterill's collection achieved widespread use. Countless collections, and hundreds of hymns, soon followed.

"Angels from the Realms of Glory" first saw the light of day in the *Iris* on Christmas Eve 1816. The path by which Montgomery's poem became linked to the tune published three decades later as *"Les anges dans nos campagnes"* is, as usual, complex and sometimes obscured by the historical undergrowth.

It is not clear which, if any, tune Montgomery intended for these words. By writing in the aptly named "common meter" (albeit with a two-line refrain added to each verse), he may have been inviting his readers to sing it to any tune they liked that happened to fit, a time-honored way of doing things. Whatever his intentions, his text proved highly popular in songbooks and ballad sheets.

Meanwhile, the appearance of the Noël *"Les anges dans nos campagnes"* in print appears to have led to a number of English translations and paraphrases. One such, "The Angels We Have Heard on High," by the Roman Catholic Bishop of Newcastle, appeared in 1860, set to a simplified version of the original French tune. This version then took on something of a life of its own, for some reason becoming part of the traditional carol repertory in the West Country.

The story now heads south to London and another in our cast of colorful Victorian characters, Henry Smart. Smart was one of the finest organists of his day, a genius in the art of congregational accompaniment, and almost totally blind. In 1867, he edited (largely by dictation to his daughter Ellen) the *Psalms and Hymns for Divine Worship*. Among the tunes is his own "Regent Square" (named after a posh bit of Regency Bloomsbury), which, it turns out, fits Montgomery's poem splendidly. The story could happily have ended here. In 1928, however, the editors of the *Oxford Book of Carols*, presumably having noticed the similarity between the opening of Montgomery's poem and the old French Noël, decided this was reason enough to graft his words on to its original tune. It doesn't fit terribly well. Why would it? The old tune was intended for words in a different language (if, indeed, it was intended for words at all).

Whatever the complex history of continental cross-pollination that led to this point, there are now several hybrids of the original tune lined up in the musical greenhouse. From here they begin to shoot off in all directions. Far from uniquely in these stories of carols, different branches of the family tree prospered on opposite sides of the Atlantic. American choirs and congregations use Smart's "Regent Square" for the words. English churches prefer the old French tune that, by a pleasingly illogical association of ideas, has become known as "Iris." (The English, incidentally, sing "Regent Square" to other words, including the mangled Victorian verbiage beginning "Light's Abode, Celestial Salem.")

And that's not the end of the matter. Far from it. For some reason the editors of the 1928 Oxford book chose not to use the simple but stirring two-line refrain with which Montgomery ends each verse. Instead they appropriated the equivalent refrain from the original Noël, which isn't in either English or French but in a third language, Latin. Neither line really works. The Latin has a different number of syllables and the lines have to be shoehorned rather awkwardly onto the extended melisma at this point in the tune. Smart's rising sequence makes much better sense of the repetition of "Come and worship." The editors had not quite got over the persistent enthusiasm for the macaronic refrain. The irony is that nothing could be less appropriate in a poem by an early nineteenth-century Scots dissenter. Montgomery would have been appalled.

Thus we find ourselves with three basic incarnations of this carol (with countless variants among and between them). In the United States, Smart's tune "Regent Square" is sung with Montgomery's words (English refrain). In the United Kingdom, the French folk tune known as "Iris" is sung with Montgomery's words (Latin refrain, usually; English refrain, sometimes). The "simplified" version of the French tune also prospers, most commonly to the words beginning "Angels we have heard on high," with many other variants including "Shepherds in the fields abiding" (which, to confuse matters further, is the first line of Montgomery's second verse, but continues quite differently).

It's the sort of intriguing muddle with which readers of this book will now be familiar. And somewhere underneath it all is the curious idea that today we find ourselves singing a tune that may, just possibly, have been one of the musical candle flames around which the gilded moths flitted and flickered at the court of Louis XIV, to words by a man who spent a good part of his career articulating the ideas that eventually brought that court to its blooded knees. Happy Christmas, Louis.

"Angels from the Realms of Glory"

An - gels, from the realms of glo - ry, Wing your flight o'er all the earth;

Ye who sang Cre - a - tion's sto - ry Now pro-claim Mes - si - ah's birth!

Come and wor - ship Christ the new-born
Glo - - - - - - ri-a in ex - cel - sis

King! Come and
De - o! Glo - - - - -

wor - ship wor - ship Christ the new - born King.
- ri - a in ex - cel - sis De - o!

Shepherds, in the fields abiding,
Watching o'er your flocks by night,
God with man is now residing,
Yonder shines the infant light:
Refrain

102

Sages, leave your contemplations,
Brighter visions beam afar;
Seek the great Desire of nations,
Ye have seen his natal star:
Refrain

Sinners, wrung with true repentance,
Doomed for guilt to endless pains,
Justice now revokes the sentence,
Mercy calls you—break your chains:
Refrain

Though an infant now we view him,
He shall fill his Father's throne,
Gather all the nations to him;
Every knee shall then bow down:
Refrain

All creation, join in praising
God the Father, Spirit, Son,
Evermore your voices raising,
To th'eternal Three in One:
Refrain

"Suddenly, There Was with the Angel a Multitude of the Heavenly Host, Praising God"

· 12 ·

"Hark, the Herald Angels Sing"

 f we think about it at all, we probably think this hymn was written by Charles Wesley (words) and Felix Mendelssohn (music). The tune is called "Mendelssohn," after all.

Well, up to a point. Although they were certainly the prime movers, so many others have had a hand in fashioning the carol as we know it today that Wesley and Mendelssohn may be regarded as not so much even *"primi inter pares"* ("first among equals") as *"pares inter pares"* ("equals among equals").

The words first. This poem is by Charles Wesley the elder, father of Methodism and of a talented, successful, and badly behaved family. Isn't it?

In fact, we get through precisely one word of Wesley's poem before we find ourselves singing alterations and interpolations added by other hands. The forensically complex process by which this hymn has mutated from Wesley's original tells us something important about Methodism and its leading early practitioners.

Hymns were their life-blood. This was an itinerant church, pioneering the concept of large-scale meetings, often held outdoors, and making long journeys on foot to spread the gospel. Stirring, striding hymns are an essential ingredient of both kinds of informal, *al fresco* worship. Charles Wesley alone is thought to have written more than six thousand, typically with ten or twenty verses each. Methodist hymnbooks and collections of verse often went through multiple editions to keep up with demand, and, just like the much-reprinted psalters of the sixteenth and seventeenth centuries, the texts evolved as they went along, no doubt partly in response to what people actually sang.

At the same time, this was a church that militated strongly against central authority. If a preacher or hymn leader wanted to emphasize or develop a particular point of doctrine, that was between him, God, and his congregation. These men could, on occasion, disagree deeply about such things. So if one of them chose to alter an existing hymn to his own purposes, nobody, least of all the original author, had the right to tell him not to. There was no copyright to be jealously guarded, and in any event, notions of individual authorship were less strongly developed. In very many cases authorship is not ascribed at all, leaving it unclear whether a hymn is by Charles or John, or both, or someone else entirely. It was, at least up to a point, understood and accepted that this is a collaborative process.

This carol, then, bears the imprint of some strong and colorful personalities.

To begin with, here is the text as Charles Wesley first published it in the 1739 edition of *Hymns and Sacred Poems*:

Hark how all the welkin rings
"Glory to the King of kings,
Peace on earth, and mercy mild,
God and sinners reconcil'd!"

Joyful all ye nations rise,
Join the triumph of the skies,
Universal nature say
"Christ the Lord is born to day!"

Christ, by highest heav'n ador'd,
Christ, the everlasting Lord,
Late in time behold him come,
Offspring of a virgin's womb.

Veil'd in flesh, the Godhead see,
Hail th' incarnate deity!
Pleas'd as man with men t' appear
Jesus, our Immanuel here!

Hail the heav'nly Prince of Peace!
Hail the Sun of righteousness!
Light and life to all he brings,
Ris'n with healing in his wings.

Mild he lays his glory by,
Born—that man no more may die,
Born—to raise the sons of earth,
Born—to give them second birth.

Come, desire of nations, come,
Fix in us thy humble home,
Rise, the woman's conqu'ring seed,
Bruise in us the serpent's head.

Starting as early as the second edition later that same year, and on through the many subsequent reprintings, small changes creep in. It was subjected to more substantial editorial attention in a 1758 volume edited by George Whitefield.

Whitefield had been a member of the Wesley brothers' "Holy Club" at Christ Church, Oxford (mockingly christened "Methodists" by their fellow undergraduates for their prim, methodical ways). He was a passionate preacher, pioneer of the mass meeting, and an intrepid traveler. His journeys took him to Bermuda, Ireland, and Gibraltar. He visited America seven times, becoming a real celebrity there. Benjamin Franklin invited Whitefield to stay in his house, and remembered: "He replied, that if I made that kind Offer for Christ's sake, I should not miss of a Reward. And I return'd, Don't let me be mistaken; it was not for Christ's sake, but for your sake."[1] Franklin also conducted a typically scientific experiment to work out how many people could comfortably hear Whitefield's "loud and clear voice" when he was preaching outside. He made it thirty thousand.

Back in England, Whitefield had a go at Wesley's opening couplet, turning

Hark, how all the welkin rings!
Glory to the King of kings.

into

Hark, the herald-angels sing,
Glory to the new-born King!

Further changes followed in 1760 at the hand of Martin Madan, priest, lawyer, Calvinist, yet another former Christ Church man and author of an embarrassingly enthusiastic treatise on polygamy.

Apart from altering some of the words, the main change in these later versions is the reduction in the number of verses, partly, perhaps, to skirt gently around some of the knottier theology about original sin and whose fault it was. By the time Sandys included "Hark, the Herald" in his collections of 1833 and 1852, there were five verses, with the opening couplet of verse one used as a refrain, just as we do today. The text has reached its modern form (except that the verses still have four lines each, as in Wesley, rather than the later eight).

Do the changes improve Wesley's hymn? Some think so. Some commentators believe that Wesley wrote so much and so quickly that he allowed bad poetry to stand alongside good, sometimes in the same work (perhaps unsurprising when your known output of hymns and other poems totals more than nine thousand). Many of his texts were edited by others for publication. He expected it. And Whitefield was only tidying up uncomfortable archaisms like *welkin*.

But, on the other hand, *welkin* is a perfectly respectable English word. Shakespeare uses it. It means the sky, the firmament, the heavens. It is, in fact, the right word for the scene of the angels' airborne performance that night. Also, the word-stress of the phrase "Hark, the herald-angels" puts the accent too much on the herald part, not the angels: "hark, the angel-heralds" would have been better. And (without getting too deep into biblical exegesis) "King of kings" is certainly more inspiring than "new-born king." It's a quote from the book of Revelation (and Handel's very-nearly contemporary *Messiah*). It separates out this king from all others, which "new-born king" does not. And there is something gloriously inclusive, almost pantheistic, something of the spirit of Addison, in Wesley's lines:

> Universal nature say
> "Christ the Lord is born today!"

Much better than Whitefield's replacement:

> With th'Angelic hosts proclaim,
> Christ is born in Bethlehem!

that doesn't rhyme and puts a whopping accent on the last syllable of *Bethlehem* (which he also does later to the word *Emmanuel* by making it a four-rather than a three-syllable word).

The Wesleys didn't like people changing their hymns. John said:

> Many gentlemen have done my brother and me (though without naming us) the honour to reprint many of our hymns. Now they are perfectly welcome so to do, provided they print them just as they are. But I desire, they would not attempt to mend them; for they really are not able. None of them is able to mend either the sense or the verse. Therefore, I must beg of them one of these two favours: either to let them stand just as they are, to take them for better for worse; or to add the true reading in the margin, or at the bottom of the page; that we may no longer be accountable either for the nonsense or for the doggerel of other men.[2]

Well, quite.

Unfortunately for Wesley senior, it doesn't matter what he begs. People sing it like this because they like it like this, and they like it because they know it. Some twentieth-century editors, including Vaughan Williams, tried to restore Wesley's welkins: congregations just laughed. Usage is sanctified by habit. Hamlet was right: "There is nothing either good or bad, but thinking makes it so."[3] Or, perhaps, not thinking.

By using four-line stanzas in a regular meter, Charles Wesley created a hymn that could be sung to a number of tunes. Candidates include "Savannah" (sung today to "Love's Redeeming Work Is Done"), which John Wesley had recently imported from the Moravians, and "Easter Hymn" from the *Lyra Davidica* book of 1708 ("Jesus Christ Is Risen Today"), complete with Alleluias, a splendidly rousing and Christmassy way to do it. Later (but pre-Mendelssohn) hymnals use "Salzburg" ("At the Lamb's High Feast We Sing" or "Songs of Thankfulness and Praise"), which is an eight-line tune.

The Mendelssohn connection came later. You can find it stated that Mendelssohn didn't like it. This is a misreading. He didn't like some other words that an English poet put to this music, and said so. But he didn't know about the Wesley connection, which was made six years after his death. And the man who made it didn't know about Mendelssohn's objection to the earlier effort.

In 1840, Mendelssohn fulfilled a commission for a cantata to mark the four-hundredth anniversary of Gutenberg's invention of movable type. Overleaf is movement two, with its solidly Germanic scoring for men's voices and brass band.

Mendelssohn's English publisher, Ewer and Company, had it translated into English by a Mr. Bartholomew. Mendelssohn wasn't impressed:

> I must repeat the wish I already expressed in my letter to Mr. Bartholomew. I think there ought to be other words to No. 2, the "Lied." If the right ones are hit at, I am sure that piece will be liked very much by the singers and the hearers, but it will never do to

sacred words. There must be a national and merry subject found out, something to which the soldierlike and buxom motion of the piece has some relation, and the words must express something gay and popular, as the music tries to do it.[1]

Mendelssohn is writing in his second language here, but choirs could still do well to try and follow his instruction to be more "soldierlike and buxom" next time they sing this tune.

In England, Mendelssohn was a superstar. He visited many times. One of his favorite musical haunts was St. Paul's Cathedral, where his old friend Thomas Attwood ("dear old Attwood") was organist. On one of his last visits, in 1847, Mendelssohn conducted the London premiere of his oratorio *Elijah*. Among the choristers was a sixteen-year-old St. Paul's Cathedral choirboy named William Hayman Cummings.

Cummings was born in Sidbury, Devon, in 1831. He sang as a boy at both St. Paul's and the Temple Church, and in adulthood was an accomplished tenor (once taking the solo in a new cantata by Arthur Sullivan, apparently at just thirty minutes' notice), professor of singing at the Royal Academy of Music, principal of the Guildhall School, and a Gentleman of the Chapel Royal. In the early part of his professional career he was organist of Waltham Abbey in Essex (Tallis's old church). The *Musical Times* takes up the story some decades later, in 1897:

> Mr. Cummings informs us that he eagerly procured everything that Mendelssohn composed as soon as it was published. While playing over the chorus in G he was at once struck by its adaptability to the words "Hark! the herald angels sing." He copied out the parts, and the tune was sung with great enthusiasm by the congregation at Waltham Abbey. He soon afterwards began to receive so many applications for manuscript copies that he took his arrangement to Messrs. Ewer and Co., who published it in 1856.[5]

A nice irony that this is the same publishing house firmly told by Mendelssohn that the tune would "never do to sacred words."[6]

The "great enthusiasm" Cummings found for his marriage of Mendelssohn and Wesley led to its inclusion in *Hymns Ancient and Modern* in 1861.

There are, of course, a number of changes between Mendelssohn's chorus and Cummings's hymn. The third verse, in the minor, has gone. The tune is extrapolated rather ingeniously from the original by following it from vocal to instrumental parts and back again in the third phrase. Cummings has smoothed out a number of dotted rhythms. Had

1. Hark, how all the Welkin rings
"Glory to the King of Kings,
"Peace on Earth & Mercy mild,
"GOD & Sinners reconcil'd!

2. Joyful all ye Nations rise,
Join the Triumph of the Skies,
Universal Nature say
Christ the Lord is born to day!

3. Christ by highest Heaven ador'd,
Christ the everlasting Lord,
Late in Time behold Him come
Offspring of a Virgin's Womb.

4. Veil'd in Flesh the Godhead see,
Hail th' Incarnate Deity,
Pleas'd as Man with Men t' appear
Jesus, our Immanuel here.

5. Hail the Heavenly Prince of Peace,
Hail the Sun of Righteousness!
Light & Life to all He brings
Ris'n with Healing in his Wings.

6. Mild He lays his Glory by,
Born, that Man no more may die,
Born, to raise the Sons of Earth,
Born, to give them second Birth.

7. Come, Desire of Nations, come,
Fix in us thy humble Home,
Rise the Woman's Conquering Seed,
Bruise in Us the Serpent's Head.

8. Now display thy Saving Power,
Ruin'd Nature now restore,
Now in mystic Union join
Thine to Ours, & Ours to Thine.

9. Adam's Likeness, Lord, efface,
Stamp thine Image in it's Place,

"Hark (etc. . . .)" in Charles Wesley's own handwriting.

he lived to do so, Mendelssohn might well have believed himself justified in echoing Wesley's wail of a hundred years before.

But at least one of the changes was neither Cummings's fault nor to his liking, as the *Musical Times* makes clear: "As Mr. Cummings justly says, an unwarrantable alteration has been made in the melody by the introduction of a B at the third beat of bar twelve which Mendelssohn did not write."[7] Cummings, mender of Mendelssohn, has been mended in his turn.

Mended or mangled, this one stuck. Words and music have passed through many hands, some unknown, to reach the familiar form we know today. They have appeared in pretty much every carol book since 1861. Mendelssohn's soldierlike and buxom paean to movable type has helped perpetuate the legacy of Johannes Gutenberg in a way he could never have foreseen.

"Hark, the Herald Angels Sing"

Christ, by highest heaven adored,
Christ, the everlasting lord
Late in time behold Him come,
Off-spring of a Virgin's womb
Veiled in flesh the Godhead see,
Hail, the incarnate deity
Pleased as Man with men to dwell,
Jesus, our Emmanuel.
Hark! the herald angels sing,
"Glory to the New-born king!"

Hail the heav'n-born Prince of Peace,
Hail, the Sun of Righteousness
Light and life to all He brings,
Risen with healing in His Wings.
Now He lays His Glory by,
Born that man no more may die
Born to raise the sons of earth,
Born to give them second birth.
Hark! the herald angels sing,
"Glory to the New-born king!"

"They Saw Mary and Joseph, and the Babe, Lying in a Manger"

"Away in a Manger"

 n a 1996 poll to find the most popular Christmas carols in the United Kingdom, "Away in a Manger" came in second.

Not bad for a youngster.

This one's only been around for about 130 years. In that time it has garnered more tunes than probably any other carol. It has also generated considerable confusion about who wrote it, a misattribution to Luther, and a minor theological controversy.

In 1884 this appeared in a Boston publication called *The Myrtle*:

Luther's Cradle Song.

Martin Luther, the great German reformer, who was born four hundred years ago the 10th of next November, composed the following hymn for his children ; and it is still sung by many German mothers to their little ones : —

Away in a manger,
No crib for his bed,
The little Lord Jesus
Lay down his sweet head.
The stars in the sky
Looked down where he lay,
The little Lord Jesus
Asleep in the hay.

The cattle are lowing,
The poor baby wakes ;
But little Lord Jesus,
No crying he makes,
I love thee, Lord Jesus :
Look down from the sky,
And stay by my crib,
Watching my lullaby.

It may be sung to the air of "Home, Sweet Home."

It's an intriguing item. For one thing, the paper states as a fact that the text is by Martin Luther. It isn't. Luther wrote lots of hymns, but he didn't write this one. Deliberately or otherwise, the editors have confidently misinformed their readers, for reasons that may or may not be connected with a series of pageants and celebrations held in Boston and the surrounding area to mark the four-hundredth anniversary of Luther's birth (which was actually a year earlier, anyway). It stuck. The hymn appeared in print many times with his name attached in the following decades, often under the unambiguous title "Luther's Cradle Hymn." Lots of children have been lulled to sleep by these words. Luther's own *neugeboren kinder* were not among them.

Another interesting feature is that the words, not untypically for a Christmas carol, are not quite as we know them today. Change has not necessarily meant improvement. The image of the Christ-child "watching my lullaby" is a touching one, perhaps better than the faux-archaic "stay by my bedside 'til morning is nigh," which has replaced it. The poem is also one syllable short in a few places, for example in line five, necessitating the later addition of the metrically regular but meteorologically questionable adjective *bright* for the night sky.

As well as no author, there is no tune. It's a fascinating thought that the editors expected their lyric to be sung to Henry Bishop's parlor song "Home! Sweet Home!" This tune, with words by the American John Howard Payne and based (according to Bishop) on a Sicilian folk song, was vastly popular in the United States. Both sides in the Civil War adopted it. Lincoln had it sung at the White House. Its message of the heartfelt peace and sanctity of the family home make it the perfect fit for this quiet little household prayer over the sleeping child. Try it. See?

Despite, or perhaps because of, this lack of an authorized melody, composers treated the text as fair game for their own inventions, inspired no doubt by the simple charm of the imagery and the gentle, rocking triple-time meter (an unusual feature: there are some traditional carol tunes with three beats to the bar or half-bar, but they tend to work by elongating the first syllable of groups of two, for example *"In dulci jubilo"* and *"Quem pastores"*). The vast majority of the specially composed tunes to "Away in a Manger" are, unlike "Home! Sweet Home!" in some version of three-time.

Then, in 1892, a third verse appeared. This, too, has been misattributed. It may well be by Charles H. Gabriel, who edited the book in which it was first printed and wrote the tune that lives with it there. Bishop William Anderson later claimed that Dr. John T. MacFarland, the secretary of his Board of Sunday Schools, wrote, at his request, the third verse for Children's Day.[1] Again, the attribution persisted, and again, it is erroneous. Anderson's publication postdated Gabriel's by more than a decade. In fact, like so many of its older brethren, it's impossible to say for certain who wrote the words.

The theological controversy centers on the line "the little Lord Jesus, no crying he makes," which has been taken by some as denying Christ the full attributes of humanity by not behaving like a real human child, a heresy known as "Docetism." This is certainly not the place to become entwined in doctrinal niceties, except perhaps to observe that this is far from the only occasion in our carol repertoire where a poet is filling in with a bit of local color of his own. The Gospels tell us almost nothing about Christ's infancy and early life, and many of its most familiar features are later inventions and embellishments, hallowed by long use: the animals peering patiently at us from inside the stable, source of inspiration alike to the greatest masters of Renaissance art and the costume ladies of the school nativity play; the three kings with their crowns and gowns; and, above all, the bleak midwinter. There are no frosty winds in Luke. And anyway, the poet doesn't say that the baby Jesus doesn't cry at all, ever—just not at this particular moment. Perhaps the lowing of the cattle distracted him. It seems a harmless enough detail.

In 1951, Richard S. Hill published a thorough and splendidly entertaining article called "Not So Far Away in a Manger," listing all the musical settings he could find. There are forty-one. Clearly there is no scope (and probably less appetite) for a comprehensive review of the whole lot here (and there are plenty more, both before and since Hill's epic feat of collation and indexing). We limit ourselves here to the two tunes sung most often in, respectively, the United Kingdom and the United States.

The biographies of the two composers are strikingly similar.

William J. Kirkpatrick was an organist, hymn writer, and one-time fife major in the Philadelphia Volunteers. He issued some one hundred books of devotional pieces, often with his business partner John R. Sweney. In 1895, they published *Around the World with Christmas. A Christmas Exercise*, a kind of Christmas play. "Away in a Manger" (under the usual title "Luther's Cradle Hymn") is "for singing by the Primary School, or selected scholar." Kirkpatrick's simple piano arrangement evokes the world of the school song and the camp meeting, with its strong, static bass and well-meaning thirds and sixths.

A nice story neatly captures something of the character of Kirkpatrick and his world. He would often attend large Methodist meetings, organizing and leading the music. On one occasion he noticed that the soloist he had engaged to lead the hymns was getting into the habit of leaving before the sermon. Concerned for the state of the young man's soul, he began to turn over the words of a new hymn in his mind:

I've wandered far away from God,
Now I'm coming home;
The paths of sin too long I've trod,
Lord, I'm coming home.
Coming home, coming home,
Nevermore to roam;
Open now Thine arms of love,
Lord, I'm coming home.

Kirkpatrick handed the young man his new lyric. Moved, the singer found himself approaching the altar and accepting the preacher's call to "come home." Kirkpatrick's tune to "Away in a Manger" has kept the name originally given to the words, "Cradle Song."

James Ramsey Murray, composer of our other tune, also served as an army musician in the Civil War period, studied the art of hymn writing with leading practitioners including the great Lowell Mason, worked in publishing and as a schoolteacher, and wrote a great many hymns. The residual German associations of this one, surface in his version. His tune bears the name "Mueller," after a certain Carl Mueller, who is credited as the composer in a number of publications but appears in fact to be not just the subject of yet another case of misattribution but entirely fictional. Some have noted a similarity (actually pretty slight), between the opening phrase of Murray's tune and part of a waltz by Johann Strauss the younger (number four of "Tales from the Vienna Woods"). Perhaps there is a nod here in the direction of the "Pennsylvania Deutsch" (or "Dutch"), the large local German population, whose attachment to their compatriot Martin Luther gave birth to this carol in the first place (and caused such confusion thereafter).

Its cradle, *The Myrtle*, was the public voice of the Universalist movement, which seeks a humanity and religion common to all. The other items on the same page convey something of the essence and flavor of the approach. An improving domestic tale ends with the tagline "Somebody stands in Christ's place in every home. Who is it in your house?" A butterfly reminds a hummingbird (who he first met when he was a caterpillar) to judge not, lest ye be judged: "Never insult the humble, as they may someday become your superiors." Some singers have found something similarly sentimental and didactic in "Away in a Manger." But there is, too, something rugged and sincere in its emotional hinterland, rooted in the faith and soul of the eastern seaboard of post–Civil War America.

In its short career, this little carol has gone through many of the life experiences of many of its older and wiser brethren. It has lost track of some of its parents, has picked up several more and less suitable partners, and spawned a number of offspring and variants. Like folk song, many of its tunes sound like variations of each other, perhaps because the placing of cadence and meter is almost a natural phenomenon, like similarities of word formation across different languages. Some of the tunes actually fit together, again, like some folk songs.

But there's an artfulness too. The words shift to the first person in the middle of the second verse, so subtly that we barely notice. Uniquely, we speak in the voice of the actual baby itself, gazing up from the crib with big, round unblinking eyes. Sentimental, certainly, but what could better evoke the sense of appealing to the protection of another baby, far away, in a manger?

It's a folk song for our times—the new old. It's a song about home, safety, and a little, tiny child, sleeping peacefully.

Home, sweet home.

"Away in a Manger"

Away in a manger, no crib for a bed,
The little Lord Jesus laid down his sweet head.
The stars in the bright sky looked down where he lay
The little Lord Jesus asleep on the hay.

The cattle are lowing, the baby awakes,
But little Lord Jesus no crying he makes.
I love thee, Lord Jesus! look down from the sky.
And stay by my bedside till morning is nigh.

Be near me, Lord Jesus, I ask thee to stay
Close by me forever, and love me, I pray.
Bless all the dear children in thy tender care,
And take us to heaven to live with thee there.

"I Wonder As I Wander"

olk songs and Christmas go together like turkey and cranberry sauce. They are as much a part of our traditional Christmas festivities as fairy lights and traffic jams.

They didn't always get there in a straight line. Sometimes the connection between folk imagery and Christmas is obscure, to say the least. Others originally had nothing to do with Christmas. Composers and clerics have draped seasonal associations all over them like tinsel on a tree.

All these songs owe their place in our repertoire to the person who first wrote them down. This, too, is not as straightforward a process as it sounds. Folk songs, by definition, exist in many different versions. They change from one village to the next, one generation to another. Which version should the collector use? What gives him (or, in some notable cases, her) the right to set one particular version in stone? By preserving the oral tradition, are we not also ending it?

On the other hand, is the collector permitted to add something, to consider his own version just one variant among many? Is he allowed to polish up a rough original, or finish something that he finds incomplete?

"I Wonder As I Wander" is an Appalachian folk song. Or, at least, a bit of it is.

The first collector to make a serious attempt to record the folk music of the Appalachian Mountains was an Englishman, Cecil Sharp. Sharp was unquestionably top of the class among collectors, a dedicated and single-minded pioneer, going out along the highways and hedges of the south and west of England and elsewhere in search of songs, dances, melodies, ballads, and anything else he could find. The huge and wonderful archive based at Cecil Sharp House in north London is his legacy.

He visited the higher reaches of the Appalachian hills stretching from Virginia to South Carolina in 1916. He didn't like it much. "It is strenuous work," he wrote. "There are no roads in our sense of the word . . . I go about in a blue shirt, a pair of flannel trousers with a belt, a Panama hat and an umbrella. The heat is very trying."[1] His vegetarianism proved a challenge in the land of the *chitlin'*, a dish made of pigs' intestines.

Many of the songs he collected are versions of English originals, presumably arrived on the eastern seaboard with settlers from the seventeenth century on, then taking on a fascinating new life of their own. There are, for example, two versions of the familiar English favorite "The Cherry Tree Carol," with both words and music given a distinctive local twang:

Then Joseph said to Mary, so rough and unkind:
Let the daddy of the baby get the cherries for thine.

Sharp was a champion and a hero of the folk movement, no question. But some also see him as a manipulator, preserving, even creating, a particular aspect of folk art to suit an agenda of his own. His Appalachian collection almost completely ignores black singers, from whom he took down just 2 of his 122 published songs. Some suspect a political motive, in the turmoil surrounding the reordering of class and society in the years around the First World War. A hilarious cine film sums up the contradictions: Sharp, performing a Morris dance, gamely hopping and skipping and waving his hankie, dressed in a three-piece tweed suit and looking as unlike an authentic rednecked son of the soil as it is possible to look. Then he forgets the steps and bumps smack into his dancing partner, nearly sending them both flying. Sharp didn't help resolve the riddle around his own motives by a clam-like secrecy about himself as a person in his voluminous diaries and writings. A biography by his long-term collaborator Maud Karpeles guards his public image equally jealously, making him out to be some kind of saint.

Sharp wasn't the only English aesthete of the first half of the twentieth century to use his art to cover up and deal with contradictions in his own psyche. Nor was he the last folk song collector to possibly push the meaning and content of a song beyond what he originally found.

John Jacob Niles trod the slopes of the Appalachians a couple of decades after Sharp had shipped his umbrella and his Panama hat back to Somerset. Unlike his great predecessor, Niles was a native. Here, he describes the part music played in his childhood:

> When I was a child growing up in Kentucky, we made what we needed. The daily life of my people at home was full of interesting snatches of music—perhaps just a single couplet and four measures of melody . . . we made our own fun, we made our own music, we even made our own instruments. When I was quite small, my father bought me a three-string dulcimer. But when I was up in my teens and wanted a bigger and better dulcimer, my father told me to get busy and make one. I've been making my own dulcimers ever since.[2]

This same hands-on, creative, practical approach applies to the music as well as the instruments it is played on. If a song exists as just a few "interesting snatches," but could potentially be "usable in an extended and adapted form," then your job as a singer is to finish it, and use it. As Niles said late in life, "As I look back across fifty years of public performances, I'm convinced that a concert singer who is not also a composer and a poet is at a definite disadvantage."[3] Other twentieth-century troubadours like Bob Dylan, Lennon and McCartney, and Jacques Brel would surely agree with that.

This creative willingness to work an incomplete original into something for practical use finds its perfect expression in "I Wonder As I Wander." Niles takes up the story:

"I Wonder As I Wander" grew out of three lines of music sung for me by a girl who called herself Annie Morgan. The place was Murphy, North Carolina, and the time was July 1933. The Morgan family, revivalists all, were about to be ejected by the police, after having camped in the town square for some little time, cooking, washing, hanging their wash from the Confederate monument, and generally conducting themselves in such a way as to be classed a public nuisance. Preacher Morgan and his wife pled poverty; they had to hold one more meeting in order to buy enough gas to get out of town. It was then that Annie Morgan came out—a tousled, unwashed blond, and very lovely. She sang the first three lines of the verse of "I Wonder As I Wander." At twenty-five cents a performance, I tried to get her to sing all the song. After eight tries, all of which are carefully recorded in my notes, I had only three lines of verse, a garbled fragment of melodic material—and a magnificent idea. With the writing of additional verses and the development of the original melodic material, "I Wonder As I Wander" came into being.[4]

Niles began including it in concerts. His own recording from 1958 provides a fascinating glimpse of the Hillbilly hinterland of this song before it put away childish things and became a pretty little church carol. He accompanies himself on the dulcimer, repeating each twangy, metal-stringed chord more or less "ad lib" as he delivers the tune in a free, improvisatory rhythm over the top, without any real metrical pulse. Typically, he exploits the extremes of vocal range by putting the tune in a high key, in this case F minor, showing off his characteristic eerie falsetto on the long, held top C in the refrain. The effect is strange, intriguing, compelling, and a million miles from any polished choir-stall or starched surplice.

The song caught on, and like so many others with their roots in the fertile soil of folk traditions, it soon entered the repertoire of "soloists and choral groups wherever the English language is spoken or sung," as Niles put it.[5]

Is it a folk song? In a sense, Niles is doing no more than any other folk musician—using the bits he and his fellow singers can remember, and making up the rest. That's how a folk tradition evolves and continues. But, at the same time, Niles was perfectly well aware of the difference between a real folk melody and a composed song, certainly as far as the legal and financial implications go. When he wrote a new melody to "Black Is the Color of My True-Love's Hair," he carefully distinguished between "my composition" and "the public-domain material," the vocabulary of a man well used to the niceties of copyright law (and adding, perhaps rather ruefully, "My composition has since been 'discovered' by many an aspiring folk-singer").[6]

Like Vaughan Williams, Niles built the cadences, the language, and the flavor of authentic folk song into his own original conceptions, and, like Vaughan Williams, it is sometimes unclear where the boundaries lie. In claiming his royalties, he is perhaps doing no more than young Annie, whose memory seems to have been mysteriously stimulated to successively greater feats of recollection by the cumulative promise of "twenty-five cents a performance." Let's hope Annie earned her family their tankful of gas out of town.

Whatever the details of who wrote what, we have a gorgeous, haunting song with the kind of lilting, modal melody and characterful, dialect-tinged lyrics that leap from every page of Sharp's monumental collection. This is the authentic voice of the Appalachian hills.

The words have that strange mixture of the voice of the English Puritan and an earthier American religious accent that appear from the early days of the *Bay Psalter* and beyond. It's often been suggested that some aspects of Elizabethan English survived in America from the language brought over on the *Mayflower* in a way that they did not in England. Here are archaisms and inversions like "come for to die" and "it then did recall." "The promise of ages" could be Cranmer. "Any wee thing" sounds curiously Scottish. At the same time, *birthed* and *on'ry* are distinctively American formations: (*orn'ry*, interestingly, has the additional dialect meaning of "cantankerous" or "cranky," as well as being an abbreviation of *ordinary*, worth remembering next time you sing it and glance round your congregation and fellow choir members).

Many genuine folk carols cover more of the life and teachings of Jesus than just the nativity. The first verse of this one, the bit Annie managed to remember, is perhaps more properly an Easter carol than a Christmas one. Then it takes off on a series of rambling reflections, as free from settling on any kind of devotional point as a "star in the sky or a bird on the wing."

We owe this lovely song to a chance encounter between a little girl and a musician of creativity and imagination. Niles and his kin across the continents and ages have preserved for us uncountable musical riches. How many Annie Morgans have wandered off into silence and darkness, their motor-car spluttering out of the town square on half a tank of gas, their washing safely retrieved from the stern statue of Silent Sam the Confederate soldier, itself long since vanished?

And how many are still out there?

"I Wonder As I Wander"

When Mary birthed Jesus 'twas in a cow's stall,
With wise men and farmers and shepherds and all.
But high from God's heaven a star's light did fall,
And the promise of ages it then did recall.

If Jesus had wanted for any wee thing,
A star in the sky, or a bird on the wing,
Or all of God's angels in heav'n for to sing,
He surely could have it, cause he was the King.

December 26: St. Stephen's Day

· 15 ·

"Good King Wenceslas"

ew carols have had so much scorn heaped on them as this poor little thing. Elizabeth Poston called it the "product of an unnatural marriage between Victorian whimsy and the thirteenth-century," which is both "bizarre" and "ridiculous."[1] Several writers have used the word *doggerel*. One went as far as calling it "ponderous moral doggerel."[2] The great Percy Dearmer expressed the pious hope that, "with the present wealth of carols for Christmas, 'Good King Wenceslas' may gradually pass into disuse."[3]

But it didn't. The fact that Dearmer and Poston were wrong tells us something important about our carol tradition.

Good King Wenceslas wasn't a king, and he wasn't called Wenceslas. But he was good, so our mythologizing lyricist scores one out of three for historical accuracy, which is probably better than some. Our hero's real name, in his native Czech, was Vaclav (Wenceslas seems to be a German version of the name), and he ruled as duke (not king) of Bohemia in the early tenth century. His family life was a trifle irregular. He was brought up by his grandmother until she was murdered by his mother, who then ruled as regent, but with such cruelty that she in turn was overthrown and exiled by Vaclav. He proved a wise and sympathetic monarch, deeply pious and dedicated to his beloved Catholic Church, building many churches and shrines, including St. Vitus's Cathedral, still standing within the walls of Prague castle. In 935 he was invited to dinner by his own brother, Boleslav, and was murdered. In a plot twist worthy of *Macbeth*, Boleslav's son was born on the very day of the murder.

There are lots of stories of Vaclav's piety and good works. The tale of the page, the peasant, and the pine-logs, of course, isn't one of them. It's fiction: one of those myths that gather around the image of a favorite saint or celebrity.

Almost a thousand years later a Victorian hymn writer and clergyman was looking for material for a new collection of carols. John Mason Neale was a prolific and popular writer. He has a whopping thirty-nine entries in the *New English Hymnal*, more than any other author, thirteen ahead of his nearest rival, Charles Wesley. Among his familiar efforts are "Jerusalem the Golden," "All Glory, Laud and Honour," "Christ Is Made the Sure Foundation," "Come, Ye Faithful, Raise the Anthem," "The Day of Resurrection," and many others. On this occasion he wanted a carol not for Christmas Day itself but for St. Stephen's Day, December 26, one of the several feast days that fall during the liturgical *octave*, the eight days following a major festival of the church year.

The story of Stephen does not really lend itself to Christmas jollity, so Neale turned instead to the legend of Vaclav, which happens to be set on the right date. The link with Christmas is already looking a bit thin. True, St. Stephen's Day is chronologically, if not liturgically, closer to Christmas than some of the events we bundle up together and sing about at Christmas (Advent, Epiphany, the Annunciation). But the Feast of Stephen has nothing to do with Christmas, and anyway the carol is not about Stephen, it's about Wenceslas, whose own feast day is in September. Any remaining tenuous link with the meaning of Christmas has been stretched almost beyond breaking point.

This was one of the reasons why the brainy chaps of English music and letters took such a dislike to Neale's carol. The other was his verse. Perhaps, at some level, they were nervous about his dangerously subversive message of social equality and redistribution of wealth. This was, after all, the age that readily got to its feet in church to heartily applaud the Almighty's good sense in putting "the rich man in his castle, the poor man at his gate, God made them high and lowly, and ordered their estate." Some found his moral tone hectoring and kitsch. Others just thought it was bad poetry. Some tried to untie his more tortured syntax. "Good my page" becomes, in some later editions, the rather more sensible "my good page." But it didn't stick. People didn't like it.

Why? Because, whether we like it or not, a certain kind of sentimental, Victorian cod-medievalism rings the right bells. Or, as Neale might have put it, the right bells ring.

But on a more serious level, there is something challenging in Neale's choice of subject matter for his carol. Wenceslas is a saint of the Catholic Church. The story Neale uses is not based on any documented incident in his life. It's a myth. There are pictures of modern-day cardinals, red-hatted and resplendent, carrying Wenceslas's one-thousand-year-old skull on a gilded cushion in procession to the altar. This is the sort of thing that the men who founded Neale's church in the sixteenth century absolutely loathed. Is there something slightly disturbing in the idea of an English cleric putting this sort of idolatry into the mouths of English choristers? His contemporaries thought so. Many were deeply distrustful of his brand of high church Anglo-Catholicism. Once he was attacked at a nun's funeral. Crowds threatened to stone him and burn down his house. His own bishop banned him from ministry for nineteen years.

For his tune, Neale turned to a book published in Finland in 1582. *Piae Cantiones ecclesiasticae velerum episcoporum* is a collection of school songs assembled by Jaako Suomalainen, headmaster of Turku cathedral school. In 1853 a British diplomat brought a copy home to London and gave it to Neale, who in turn shared it with his friend and fellow high-churchman Thomas Helmore, and forth they went together through the task of translating the texts, transcribing the musical notation, and turning the results into suitably Victorianized choral arrangements, like some half-forged antique or bad bit of Gilbert Scott.

Few collaborations have produced such a concentration of repertoire items. Among their Christmas hymns are "O Come, O Come, Emmanuel," "Of the Father's Love Begotten," "A Great and Mighty Wonder," "Good Christian Men, Rejoice" (*"In dulci jubilo"*), "Unto Us Is Born a Son" (*"Puer nobis nascitur"*), "Gabriel's Message Does Away" (*"Angelus emittitur"*), "Christ Was Born on Christmas Day" (*"Resonet in laudibus"*), "Let the Song Be Begun" (*"Personent hodie"*), and many others. Within the manner of their age, Neale and Helmore were scholars, and brought much of the writing and music of the early and eastern churches back into the light of day. They virtually invented the modern use of plainsong.

Jaako Suomalainen, the singing headmaster in the sixteenth-century snows of Finland, used his songbook as a vehicle for moral as well as musical instruction. This was a deeply Protestant notion, a flame still burning resolutely in the England of three centuries later. In 1854, Neale issued his carols in a "condensed" version for children, and several other books aimed at young people. Others did the same. The carol we know as "Infant Holy, Infant Lowly," for example, was imported from its native Poland by Edith M. Reed and published in *Primary Education: A Monthly Journal for Primary Teachers*, vol. XXVIII, no. 10, December 1920. Same idea: turn an exotic original into a polite English carol with a neat moral and a nice tune, though no doubt Neale's Finnish lacked a certain polish.

Neale took the tune for "Good King Wenceslas" unaltered from the *Piae Cantiones*. The tune probably predates the book by about three hundred years. On this occasion, unlike his other gleanings from the *Cantiones*, Neale chose not to translate the original words. Easy to work out why. *"Tempus adet floridum"* is a secular song about spring. Another version of this poem, from the *Carmina Burana* of the eleventh to the thirteenth centuries, goes into rather more detail about some of the activities traditionally associated with that time of year, principally among priests and virgins, apparently. Neale would have turned away a blushing eye.

It's a great tune. Elizabeth Poston thinks it sounds better sung as intended, as an earthy spring song, stamping your feet and playing the hurdy-gurdy. She has a point. The quirky melisma in the last bar (*fu-u-el*, etc.), which gives the last line the wrong number of beats, sounds as if it is inviting the singer to hurl his glass of schnapps skyward toward the roof-tree. But, not for the first time, an English clergyman decided to press a rambunctious old tune into the service of higher things.

"Good King Wenceslas" is a song. Just another winter's tale. It may be only distantly related to Christmas, but it has the warm glow of a nice moral and a rousing tune, and it's snowing. That'll do. Our carols may not all turn out exactly as the grown-ups intended, but we can still love them for what they are.

"Good King Wenceslas"

Good King Wen-ces-las looked out on the feast of Ste-phen,

When the snow lay round a-bout, deep and crisp and e-ven.

Bright-ly shone the moon that night, though the frost was cru-el,

When a poor man came in sight, gath'ring win-ter fu-el.

"Hither page and stand by me,
If thou know'st it, telling,
Yonder peasant, who is he?
Where and what his dwelling?"
"Sire, he lives a good league hence.
Underneath the mountain;
Right against the forest fence,
By Saint Agnes' fountain."

141

"Bring me flesh, and bring me wine,
       Bring me pine-logs hither:
    Thou and I will see him dine,
       When we bear them thither."
Page and monarch forth they went,
       Forth they went together;
Through the rude wind's wild lament,
       And the bitter weather.

    "Sire, the night is darker now,
       And the wind blows stronger;
    Fails my heart, I know now how,
       I can go no longer."
"Mark my footsteps, good my page;
       Tread thou in them boldly;
    Thou shalt find the winter's rage
       Freeze thy blood less coldly."

    In his master's steps he trod,
       Where the snow lay dinted;
    Heat was in the very sod
       Which the saint had printed.
Therefore, Christian men, be sure,
       Wealth or rank possessing,
    Ye who now will bless the poor,
       Shall yourselves find blessing.

December 28: Holy Innocents

· 16 ·

"Personent hodie"

PS: LXXXIX.

M Isericordias DOMINI in æternum cantabo, in generatione & generationem, annunciabo veritatem tuam in ore meo.

It may appear slightly incongruous that one of the principal sources of English Christmas carols originated in Finland. The explanation lies in that most potent force in the shaping of human destinies: luck. The fact that this particular book survived, came into the possession of a couple of English clergymen, who then used it as a source for their own carol book, which in its turn survived and prospered, is the result of a series of coincidences and chance encounters.

There is no particular significance in the Finnish connection. There is no evidence that Father Christmas owned a copy, nor that it was nibbled by reindeer. This kind of song collection, mostly but not exclusively moral or devotional in character, was hugely popular in the European Renaissance period, part of the explosion of interest in education and ideals of behavior, fueled by the entrepreneurs of the new science of printing. There were thousands of such books. Most have vanished. Some will no doubt unvanish: *Carmina Burana*, perhaps one thousand years old, lay undiscovered in a German monastery until the late nineteenth century. There are similar examples in all fields of music and literature. More are certainly waiting patiently to be excavated from library shelf and rood loft.

Singing is a Protestant habit. Like so many similar publications, *Piae Cantiones* begins with an earnest reminder that music exists to turn the mind *"ad cogitationem rerum divinarum"* (or, as the contemporary Englishman Thomas Morley put it, "to draw the hearer by the ears, as it were in chains of gold, to the consideration of holy things"[1]). The Lutheran church put down deep and lasting roots in Scandinavia in the years around the publication of the *Piae Cantiones* in 1582. But at the time the old ways had not quite given up the ghost. Some of the texts are frankly Catholic in flavor, including two beautiful, tender settings of the *Ave Maris Stella*.

Above all, it's a book of tunes. People like tunes. Suomalainen and his printer, Theodoric Petri of the district of Nyland, knew their market. Other editions followed, in Latin, Finnish, and Swedish, new songs added along the way to maximize sales. They would surely have been thrilled, and probably rather astonished, to hear so many of their songs being lustily bellowed out by English carolers four centuries later, as a direct result of their book. Here are *"Gaudete," "Resonet in laudibus,"* *"In dulci jubilo"* (macaronic, but not as we know it, flitting fascinatingly between Latin and old Swedish), *"Puer nobis nascitur," "Personent hodie,"* *"Tempus adet floridum"* (which we know as "Good King Wenceslas"), and the tunes we sing as "Up, Good Christen Folk and Listen" and "Of the Father's Heart Begotten," among others. There is something thrilling about seeing these familiar tunes emerging from the square wooden typeface of Theodoric's press.

The book includes a few songs in two and four parts. There is a

"Passion" setting and some good Old Testament blood and thunder (*"Judith fortis, Hester mortis"*). It's the sort of musical mixture of practicality and piety that would have been instantly familiar to young men and maidens, old men and children, all over Protestant Europe.

ver nobis nafcitur Rector angelorum

gelorū, In hoc mundo panditur Dominus Do-

mi norum   ij

In præfcpe pofitum Sub fœno afinorum
Cognouerunt Dominum Chriftum Regem cœlorum.
Hunc Herodes timuit Magno cum tremore,
In infantes irruit Hos cædens in furore.
Qui natus ex Maria Die hodierna
Duc nos tua gratia Ad gaudia fuperna.
Te faluator α & ω Cantemus in choro,
Cantemus in organo, Benedicamus Domino.

Headmaster Suomalainen included some old favorites to get his pupils singing their little blond heads off. Like Luther and Calvin and their English outriders, the singing Finns pinched the best tunes they could find from the devil, the pope, the pub, and from nowhere in particular. *"Personent hodie"* is probably one of the oldest, a good example of how a tune already weathered and seasoned by time made its way to Finland, on from there through the centuries to the choir stalls of Victorian England, and, eventually, to us. It is one of the very few carols we still regularly sing in Latin, and probably the oldest in which we sing tune and words as they were originally published together. Most of our carols consist of new words grafted onto old tunes, or vice versa, or both. Not this one.

The tune first appears in a written source in Germany in 1360, implying that it was already current then and thus probably of even older origin. Like others in the *Piae Cantiones*, the tune betrays its roots in the medieval dance-carol by a vigorous swagger that almost forces you to your feet to stamp the snow off your boots and freeze your blood less coldly. The gloriously wonky metrical pattern and rhyme scheme are unique and irresistible. Most striking is the repetition of a single syllable in line six (*et de vir-, vir-, vir-,* etc.).

The modern scholars Andrew Parrott and Hugh Keyte have an explanation for this engaging musical oddity. The text appears to be a version of an earlier poem in honor of St. Nicholas, which begins *"Intonent hodie voces ecclesiae."* Nicholas, Bishop of Myra and the provinces, was also patron saint of children and among other notable achievements brought back to life three boys who had drowned (or, depending on which version you read, been murdered then pickled). In the interests of equality, Nicholas went on to rescue three girls from a life of prostitution. In the earlier text, the repeated syllable coincides with mentions of the lucky children (*"submersum,-sum,-sum puerum," "Reddens vir-, vir-, virginibus"*). The threefold repetition thus represents the three children each time. Perhaps there were some actions to go with it, a sort of mini–morality play or liturgical drama, or maybe a kind of counting song.

The link with children survives in the *"voces puerulae"* of the 1582 version. So does the repeated syllable, even though the immediate putative textual reason for it has been left behind. But note carefully what the page of music actually says at this point in the tune. The first appearance of the repeated syllable, *et de vir-*, has three repeated notes, as expected. The second, at the end of the line, quite clearly only has two. The syllable is sung first thrice, then twice, then once. Some later editors (but not all) changed it so that repetitions one and two are the same length, making a nice, regular little sequence. This is how we sing it today. Easier, maybe, but the tune has certainly lost some of its lopsided charm. (Note also that, rather sweetly, the printer has left out some of the words in the second verse, and someone has had to insert them over the top in pen.)

To find out how and why this wonderful melody has evolved and emigrated, the trail moves off-piste somewhat, to Stockholm and Queen Victoria's Minister in Residence, G. J. R. Gordon. By the 1850s, copies of the *Cantiones* were extremely rare. Gordon was presented with a copy that had belonged to Peter of Nyland, and in turn gave it to Neale and Helmore. They respectively edited and arranged the music, and translated or replaced the words. The result was two books, *Carols for Christmas-tide* of 1853, and *Carols for Easter-tide* of 1854. Each book contained twelve numbers, and the contents of both were later combined in a single, simplified version. European scholars worked on the *Cantiones* in the 1880s, and another English clergyman, George R. Woodward, produced an excellent edition of the whole book in 1910, using a kind of halfway notation combining the old square noteheads with modern clefs.

"Personent hodie" from Piae Cantiones

Their instinct for a good tune started the transfusion of much wonderful music into the bloodstream of the English carol singer. The title of the first published English version is significant. Neale and Helmore really did give us carols for "Christmas-tide," not just for Christmas. We have already seen the (rather dodgy) link between "Good King Wenceslas" and Boxing Day, December 26. *Personent hodie*, with its evocation of children singing, has become associated with December 28, the Feast of the Holy Innocents, and with the Epiphany, January 6, where it fits with the tradition of St. Nicholas bringing gifts to children on that day. We can still just catch the vinegary aroma of pickled boy hovering vaguely around this carol.

Neale also kicked off the favorite sport of coming up with English words for this tune. Poets and hymn writers have been unable to resist the challenge of finding rhymes to match the short lines and short syllables, and have had particular fun with the repeated word, or bit of word. Neale's own version begins (appropriately) "Let the song be begun." Holst's pupil Jane Marian Joseph published (under the pseudonym James M. Joseph) a well-known translation beginning "On this day earth shall ring, with the song children sing, to the Lord, Christ our King." Elizabeth Poston begins by rhyming at the half-line: "Let the boys' cheerful noise," but soon gives it up: "sing today none but joys." Most translators cheat slightly at the end, treating the last few lines as a refrain, which they most certainly aren't in the original. Some even lapse pseudo-macaronically back into Latin at this point, which is perhaps to duck the issue.

Neale keeps the original number of appearances of the repetitious monosyllable:

Sing of joy, joy, joy,
Sing of joy, joy,
Earth and skies, Bid it rise,
Gloria in excelsis.

So does Woodward, in 1910:

Et de vir-, vir-, vir-,
Et de vir-, vir-,
Et de virgineo ventre procreates

Holst made a splendid arrangement in 1916 (sometimes known as "Theodoric," taken by some authorities to be a reference to Holst's middle name, Theodore, but surely also a friendly nod to the printer of Hyland). The syllable has sprouted a sixth sibling:

Ide-o,-o,-o,
Ide-o,-o,-o,
Ideo Gloria in excelsis Deo

Joseph uses this same Latin refrain in her English version, complete with the spurious extra syllable stuck in the middle like a carrot on the face of a snowman.

F. Pratt Green's more recent version begins, "Long ago, prophets knew, Christ would come, born a Jew," and imaginatively turns the repeated syllable (including the spare) into a peal of bells:

Ring, bells, ring, ring, ring!
Sing, choirs, sing, sing, sing!
When he comes,
When he comes,
Who will make him welcome?

Piae Cantiones is a gem. We owe Neale and Helmore an incalculable debt for resurrecting these songs for us. Quite properly, they did so according to the mores of their age. We are perhaps entitled to begin to respectfully scrape off the Victorian varnish and rediscover this wonderful music for ourselves.

"Personent hodie"

Per - so - nent   ho - di - e   vo - ces pu - e - ru - lae,   lau - dan - tes

iu - cun - de   qui no - bis est   na - tus,   sum - mo De - o   da - tus,

et   de   vir,   vir,   vir,   et   de   vir,   vir,   et   de

vir - gi - ne - o   ven - tre   pro - cre - a - tus.

In mundo nascitur,

pannis involvitur

praesepi ponitur

stabulo brutorum,

rector supernorum.

perdidit,-dit,-dit,

perdidit,-dit,

perdidit spolia princeps infernorum.

Magi tres venerunt,

parvulum inquirunt,

Bethlehem adeunt,

stellulam sequendo,

ipsum adorando,

aurum, thus, thus, thus,

aurum, thus, thus,

aurum, thus, et myrrham ei offerendo.

151

Omnes clericuli,
pariter pueri,
cantent ut angeli:
advenisti mundo,
laudes tibi fundo.
ideo,-o,-o,
ideo,-o,
ideo gloria in excelsis Deo.

January 1

· 17 ·

"Here We Come a-Wassailing"

assail songs are probably the oldest, most numerous, most widespread, and most varied of all our types of carol. Just as in the language itself, bits of Anglo-Saxon, Anglo-Norman, Anglo-Roman, and Anglo-everything-else bob around in them like apples in a wassail cup. They are defiantly pagan, part fertility rite, part corporate village ritual: an incantation to the spirits of New Year and Old Twelfth Night.

Because there are so many wassail songs, separating out one individual for special attention is almost meaningless. It's like trying to spot a single tree in a vast, ancient forest.

The version given here only appears in this exact form late in the nineteenth century. But its imagery, its ideas, and its rhythm, are part of a shared memory that goes back a millennium or more. Tracing some tiny part of this rich history can, perhaps, usefully be attempted by starting at the beginning of the poem, and, thus, more or less at the beginning of musical time.

"Here we come a-wassailing . . ."

Here we come a-what? What is a wassail? And how do you come a-doing it?

The word itself is Old Norse in origin, found in Old English as *Wæs þu hæl*. It's a toast: "Be thou healthy." The response is *"Drinc hæl"*—the liquid components of this tradition were sloshed into the mix early. It probably predates the arrival of Christianity in Northern Europe.

Writing in about 1140, Geoffrey of Monmouth has this account of the meeting in the fifth century between the warrior Vortigern and the maid Rowenne: *"flexis genibus lingua Saxonica ait 'Washail, Lauert King'"* ("bending her knee, she said in the Saxon language 'Washail, Lord King'"). Vortigern, not understanding, is told: "Your answer must be "Drinchail!'" and, "from that time to this, it has been the custom in Britain, that he who drinks to anyone says 'Washail!' and he that answers says 'Drinchail!'"[1] There are several accounts of this meeting. One refers to Britain as "the land of Wassail and Drinchail."

At the coronation of William of Normandy on Christmas Day 1066, his entourage cheered their new monarch in French, leading to a fight with the locals. Nearly a century later another new king, Henry II, and his glamorous queen, Eleanor of Aquitaine, were acclaimed in two languages, but this time it was Latin and Middle English: *"Ave Rex!"* *"Wes hael!"* English was fighting back.

In the early thirteenth century, this friendly bit of English good cheer made it into what is perhaps our very earliest written carol. Significantly, the phrase is dropped into a poem written in the formal language of court and law, Norman French, which is studded with Latinisms like *quere* for *seek*:

Seignors, ore entendez à nus,
De loinz sumes venuz à wous
Pur quere Noel . . .
. . . Si jo vus di trestoz, Wesseyl!
Debaiz ait qui ne dirra Drincheyl!

Edith Rickert gives this translation:

Lordings, listen to our lay—
We have come from far away
To seek Christmas . . .
. . . Here then I bid you all *Wassail*,
Cursed be he who will not say *Drinkhail*.

". . . among the leaves so green . . ."

Lots of carols take place outside. Why this one?

It's all to do with apples.

There is a ceremony that still persists in parts of Gloucestershire and elsewhere. It's called the "Orchard-visiting Wassail." Groups of villagers are led by a Wassail king and queen to the orchard, drinking and singing as they go. The queen is lifted into the branches of the tree where she places a piece of toast soaked in a boozy apple-flavored beverage. An incantation is recited, then the villagers make as much noise as they can, shouting and banging pots and pans together, until someone discharges a gun into the branches (making sure the queen has safely descended first), to chase away evil spirits and encourage the tree to produce a good harvest next year. Sometimes the drink is tipped down into the roots. Another variant is called "howling," and involves whacking the tree with sticks.

Naturally, there are plenty of songs and rhymes to go with the ceremony, like this one:

> Old apple tree, we'll wassail thee,
> And hoping thou wilt bear.
> The Lord does know where we shall be
> To be merry anither year.

It's the sort of semi-theatrical, semi-pagan ritual that flourished before the Reformation. The authorities in the later sixteenth century, businessmen as much as Puritans, preferred their artisans and journeymen to do their praying in church and spend the rest of the week working. In 1566, Fordwich in Kent owned a splendid set of costume "appertaynyng to the kyng & the Quene of fordwiche." In 1576, the town was told to end this "superstycious or old custome . . . maynteyned vnder collour of boyes pastyme," and the "apparell & other thinges of the late supposed kinge & Quene"[2] were sold.

> **. . . here we come a-wandering,**
> **So fair to be seen,**
> **Love and joy come to you . . .**

Related to, but distinct from, the Orchard-visiting wassail is the House-visiting wassail. Villagers knock on their neighbors' door and offer to sing if they get food or money in return (or, depending on how you look at it, threaten to sing if they don't). The *Gentleman's Magazine* of 1791 relates how wassailers turn up at "the house, the doors of which they are sure to find booted by the females, who, be the weather what it may, are inexorable to all entreaties to open them till some one has guessed at what is on the spit, which is generally some nice little thing, difficult to hit on, and is their reward of him who first names it. The doors are then thrown open, and the lucky clod pole receives the tit-bit as his recompense."[3]

". . . and to you your wassail too . . ."

As well as the greeting and the visiting ceremonies, the word *wassail* also came to refer to the drink itself. It's made with apples, naturally enough, soused in a base of mulled mead or beer, spiced with sugar, ginger, nutmeg, and cinnamon, heated and decanted into a specially made bowl with sops of toast floating on top. Yum.

Other recipes include roasted crab. A variety using baked apples is known as "Lamb's Wool," as in Robert Herrick's poem "Twelfth Night":

> Next crowne the bowle full
> With gentle Lambs wooll,
> Adde sugar, nutmeg, and ginger,
> With store of ale too,
> And thus ye must doe
> To make the Wassaile a swinger.

It sounds like this wassail was certainly going to be a "swinger" (though it's interesting to speculate how, or whether, our sozzled carrolers made *swinger* rhyme with *ginger*).

Needless to say, the name "Lamb's Wool" defies explanation. It may be something to do with the pungent white froth exhaled by this particular brew. Others prefer to see it as a corruption of *La Mas Ubhal*, apple day, pronounced "lamasool" and corrupted to "lamb's wool."

". . . and God bless you
And send you a Happy New Year . . ."

The refrain of our carol places it not at Christmas but at New Year. It takes its place alongside the Lords of Misrule, boy bishops, Twelfth Night revels, and traditions of gift giving loosely linked to the Three Kings. But there is far from unanimous agreement about which date is intended. Some use January 1, others Twelfth Night, or the Eve of the Feast of the Epiphany (the end of Christmas), January 5. But, when England (finally) switched from the Julian to the Gregorian calendar in 1752, eleven days were missed out. Wednesday, September 2, 1752, was followed by Thursday, September 14, 1752, so the day that fell exactly 365 days after Twelfth Night 1752 was called not January 5, 1753, but January 17. Diehards thought this was the "true" Twelfth Night, and January 17 continues to be the favored date for wassailing in many parts of the West Country, where it is known as "Old Twelfth Night."

". . . Our wassail cup is made
Of the rosemary tree . . ."

Here is yet another meaning for our little Anglo-Saxon word: the cup or bowl from which the "wassail" drink is shared. It's large, round, and made of some suitably flavorless native wood. This is from the "Gloucestershire Wassail," nicely contrasting the colors of the various components:

Wassail! wassail! all over the town,
Our toast it is white and our ale it is brown;
Our bowl it is made of the white maple tree;
With the wassailing bowl, we'll drink to thee.

Maple sounds a better bet, on both flavor and carpentry grounds, than rosemary, which doesn't normally produce much in the way of timber.

More elaborate wassail cups are made in silver, like a "loving cup." Some have a spout, or several, so that when you drink from one you get drenched from another, which apparently adds to the fun.

At this point our modest little word takes on yet another shade of meaning. The Orchard-visiting wassail developed an indoor incarnation, where a plant or a small tree in a pot would be hung with decorated apples and the traditional pieces of doused toast. From here, tree decorations generally and baubles in particular become known as "wessel cups." The Yorkshire poet, Fred Hirst, born in 1917, has this:

Ta decorate t' Christmas tree, we'd asked mi Mam afooahr,
This pahrticulahr time she couldn't stand it nooah mooahr.

She fetched it dahn from upstairs, Wessel cups an' all,
On t' table she stood it; it wor abaht three feet tall.

Silver tinsel, all ovver t' branches wo spread,
Wessel cups wo gold, silver an' some wo red.[4]

This usage is recorded all over Yorkshire. In Bradford it's "Wesleybobs."

Another local variant is the "Gooding Carol," where the widows of the parish would go "Gooding" or "Thomasing" (or "Tommying"), collecting alms on St. Thomas's Day, December 21, the shortest day of the year. The carol is also known as the "Wessel Cup Carol."

". . . We are not daily beggars
That beg from door to door;
But we are neighbours' children,
Whom you have seen before . . ."

This carol is full of social protocol. The wassailers are always keen to stress their status as neighbors, not the feared itinerant vagabonds, tinkers, or minstrels, and thus stake their claim to the local squire's charity. Almost every version of this carol notes the social divide between the master and the mistress with their butler wearing a golden ring, and the "poor children . . . wandering in the mire."

Perhaps unsurprisingly, there are plenty of accounts of these encounters spilling over into confrontation or worse. "We want a little of your money" can be sung as a benign request for pennies, or as something rather more sinister. Plenty of commentators have noticed that the practice of demanding goods with menaces has migrated into the imported American habit of "trick-or-treat."

Wassail songs are an interesting example of how the geographical spread of folk songs is linked to agriculture. This type of song grows best in the warm, hilly, rainy areas of the west and southwest of England, just like apples. Erik Routley notes that folk song, and folk carols in particular, are linked to farming areas. His "folk song belt" runs diagonally across England from Cornwall to Yorkshire. Cumberland is "no use at all." It's partly cause and effect: there are lots of songs in the West Country, so Cecil Sharp went there, so we have lots of songs from the West Country. There's also an element of chance: Baring-Gould researched the "Songs of the West" partly because he inherited an estate in Devon. The prevalence of tunes (though not specifically carols) from Surrey, is, according to Routley, "not unconnected with the fact that Dr. Vaughan Williams lived many years at Dorking."[5]

Wassail songs come from everywhere. They are about everything: society, singing, dressing up, climbing trees, neighborliness, and not starving. They're about kings, queens, and moldy cheese. They are certainly about drinking. They encompass costumes, customs, songs, recipes, dances, and decorations. The many varied spellings and renderings of the word itself hint at just how deep its associations go.

Above all, these songs are a celebration of life itself, of preservation and renewal.

God bless you, and Happy New Year.

"Here We Come a-Wassailing"

Here we come a was - sail-ing A - mong the leaves so green,
Here we come a wan - d'ring So fair___ to be seen. Love and joy come to
you, And to you your was-sail too, And God bless you and send___ you a
hap - py New Year, and God send you a hap - py New Year.

Our wassail cup is made
Of the rosemary tree,
And so is your beer
Of the best barley.
Refrain

We are not daily beggars
That beg from door to door,
But we are neighbours' children
Whom you have seen before.
Refrain

Good Master and good Mistress,
As you sit by the fire,
Pray think of us poor children
Are wandering in the mire.
Refrain

We have a little purse
Made of ratching* leather skin;
We want some of your small change
To line it well within.
Refrain

Call up the Butler of this house,
Put on his golden ring;
Let him bring us a glass of beer,
And the better we shall sing.
Refrain

Bring us out a table,
And spread it with a cloth;
Bring us out a mouldy cheese,
And some of your Christmas loaf.
Refrain

God bless the Master of this house,
Likewise the Mistress too;
And all the little children
That round the table go.
Refrain

---

* Ratching is leather that will stretch.

January 5: Twelfth Night

"The Twelve Days of Christmas"

hall we make the welkin dance indeed? Shall we rouse the night-owl . . . ?"

Shakespeare knew all about Twelfth Night. His play is basically one long party. Sir Toby Belch and Sir Andrew Aguecheek are the Lords of Misrule, the descendants of the midwinter household gods of the Roman, of Bacchus and Terpsichore.

"On the twelfth day of December!" bellows Sir Toby, as muddled about what day it is as he is about the time of night.

Would we have recognized his tune to these words?

Twelfth Night had long been one of the principal festivities of the Christmas season. At the court of Henry VIII it far outdid Christmas Day as a household knees-up, with masques, dances, morality plays with songs and scenery, and gift giving echoing the shadowy presence, somewhere off-stage, in the wings, of the shades of wise men and St. Nicholas. Sir Toby quotes "Three Merry Men Be We," a song no doubt well known to the boozy groundlings, evoking the "three-men's songs" (or "free-men's songs") of early Tudor songbooks. Party songs—rough, carefree, designed to sound better sung drunk.

But Shakespeare is writing in the death throes of this festive tradition. There is something desperate and sad in Sir Andrew and Sir Toby's manic partying, as if trying to keep something at bay: "'tis too late to go to bed now." It is significant that when Malvolio tries to make them shut up, Sir Toby spits at him that he's "a puritan." This kind of midwinter merrymaking is on the way out. The theater itself, the "great globe," is under attack. Our revels now are ended.

But something of the generous spirit of the twelve-day holiday survives in this sprightly carol, even if nowadays we do Christmas in the wrong order. We put our decorations up and file dutifully into our carol services during Advent, or even earlier. Christmas effectively ends, rather than begins, on December 25. In earlier days, and still in many traditions, gifts are given on Boxing Day, or through to the twelfth day of Christmas. This is the spirit still captured in this song. Twelfth Night, for us, is the day decorations come down (if they haven't already fallen behind the TV), the day we sweep up pine needles and broken bits of bauble and try to pretend the days are getting longer. Herrick, in the seventeenth century, talks of household decorations of holly and yew coming down at Candlemas, February 2, when the infant Jesus was presented to the world.

Christmas carols cover many different seasonal festivities and come in many different types. "The Twelve Days of Christmas" is a "numeral" carol, itself a subset of a species of folk song, counting songs.

There are lots of these (count them): "Green Grow the Rushes-oh"; "Ten Green Bottles"; "Five Little Monkeys"; "One Man Went to Mow"; "This Old Man"; "One, Two, Buckle My Shoe": "One, Two, Three, Four, Five, Once I Caught a Fish Alive"; "Ten in a Bed"; "One Potato, Two Potato"; etc. Some count down, some up. Some are in dialect, like *Yan, Tan, Tethera, Methera, Pimp,*" Cumbrian words for *one, two, three, four, five.* Cumulative rhymes with a similar structure include "This Is the House That Jack Built"; "There Was an Old Woman Who Swallowed a Fly"; "My Gran Went to Market"; and countless others.

They're games. You can sing them in the playground, walking down the street, or on a boring bus journey. You can use them as "forfeit" games, where the first person to stumble over the ever-growing list of goodies has to drop out, or give someone a treat or a kiss. They're inclusive: any number of people can join in. They're good for concentration and teamwork, and they also, of course, help teach young children to count, forward or backward (or both), sometimes with an element of spelling or linguistics thrown in (where the objects accumulate in alphabetical or some other order).

Religion uses numbers in its imagery a lot. There are three ships, three kings, three persons, four evangelists, ten commandments, and twelve disciples. There are obvious possibilities for counting songs with a devotional tinge.

"Green Grow the Rushes" places the four "gospel makers" alongside the "lily-white boys, clothed all in green," as if both are figures carved into English mythology, as indeed they are, like the Green Man grinning incongruously at us from many a church corbel and plinth, impishly eye-balling a worried-looking saint or virgin on the next pillar along. The four evangelists appear again in the haunting "Matthew, Mark, Luke and John, Bless the Bed That I Lie On." The "Seven Joys" of Mary make a gorgeous song. In other versions her joys are ten, or five, or twelve. There are twelve apostles, twelve months of the year, twelve "points," and twelve articles.

Gifts given over a twelve-day period clearly fit this kind of song perfectly.

The song, in turn, lends itself to infinite local adaptation. There are versions from Alabama ("ten mules braying"), New England ("guns shooting, bears chasing, men hunting"), Scotland ("goldspinks, plovers, and a papingo-aye"), and many other invasive species. Even within England the gifts and their order keep changing. In the very many versions found between 1780 and 1909, the first seven gifts stay pretty much the same (with the notable exception of the "calling-birds," which are, variously, collie, colley, colly, Corley, curley, colored, and canary birds, most of which are terms for a blackbird). One version has "squabs a-swimming" instead of swans, which are baby pigeons and can't swim. From verse eight upward singers swap, substitute, and generally muddle up the rest of the gifts, including "boys a-singing," "ships a-sailing," "lads a-louping," instead of "lords a-leaping," "hounds a-running," and "badgers baiting."

Much analysis has gone into the symbolism of all of this, perhaps sometimes searching for meaning that may actually not be there. It might really just be a list of things seen around the farmhouse and the village.

None of the gifts has received such attention as the first. Is the dumpy little partridge part of the aviary of medieval icons, which includes the "soft, self-wounding pelican" and "the carnal and the crane"? If so, why is it in a tree? The RSPB informs us that this is "strictly a ground bird, never likely to be found in pear trees."

Here is one attractive possible explanation. The best early source of this song is a little children's songbook called *Mirth Without Mischief,* printed in 1780. The words are much as we know them today.

Across the Channel there is a popular *chanson enfantine* called "*Les douze mois de l'année.*" The song has the same cumulative structure and a rhythmically similar melody to its English *confrère,* the gifts, interestingly, spread over the twelve months of the year rather than the twelve days of Christmas: "*deux tourterelles, trois ramiers au bois,*" up to "*onze beaux garcons*" and "*douze demoiselles gentilles et belles.*"

A brief etymological diversion. According to Greek mythology, the first partridge was created when Daedalus threw his nephew off a tower. The nephew was called Perdix. The ornithological name for the Grey Partridge is *Perdix perdix.* The French derivation from this is *perdrix.* The alternative name for our children's song is "*La Perdriole,*" "The Little Partridge."

We have our pear tree. It's a *perdrix.* It's a half-remembered mistranslation, or, perhaps, a misremembered half-translation, giving us, oddly, not one partridge up a tree, but two, both on the ground. One English, one French. A partridge *et un perdrix.*

Voilà.

Here's another intriguing possibility. At least one version has as the first gift not the familiar partridge, but "part of a juniper tree." Look how closely the syllables of the two alternative lines, vowels and consonants, match up:

And a part-ri-i-dgein apeartree
And a part of aju-ni-pertree

The partridge, from "Mirth without mischief," 1780

Given the way an oral tradition works, it is entirely plausible that one is a garbled version of the other. If so, which is the original? Juniper has its ancient and hallowed place among traditional decorative midwinter greenery. Perhaps it came first. Someone heard it wrong, sang it back as a partridge, everyone laughed, and it stuck. It's a mistake, a happy accident by an inattentive toddler or a deaf grandma.

Sometimes we have "a merry partridge in the barley," probably a more sensible place for it to forage and roost. There are many, many other versions.

Like the little 1780 book, most printed versions don't include a melody. Unsurprisingly, folk-song collectors found it sung to a whole host of tunes round the country, from Devon to Northumbria and beyond. Cecil Sharp alone noted at least seven. Some are clearly related; others are distinct items in their own right.

One thing most of the tunes have in common is that "five gold rings" (or "golden rings," or "five, a golden ring") is sung to the same snatch of melody as all the other gifts from five up. Our little flourish and *fermata* at this point is a later addition.

Step forward a middleweight Wagnerian baritone and minor composer, Frederick Austin. "Minor" is right. No composer has ever achieved so many worldwide performances over such a long period from such a small surviving output: four notes.

Austin was a musician of some substance. He sang Elgar for Elgar and Schoenberg to Schoenberg. He sang in Beecham's *Ring* and Richter's *Tannhäuser*. He premiered works by composers from Cyril Scott to Vaughan Williams. He edited *The Beggar's Opera*. Henry Wood, who conducted Austin's symphonic "Rhapsody," said that Austin was the only man who could sing Delius's *Sea Drift "con amore."*

In 1909 Austin published an arrangement of "The Twelve Days of Christmas." In it, he added his own little phrase at "five gold rings," ornamenting the last appearance with a twiddly little cadenza of the sort he no doubt sang himself, *con amore,* around the piano at Edwardian *soirées.* His version, sans cadenza, stuck in the public mind. Austin gave us the song we know today (and, in the process, gave us the small problem of a non-copyright folk song with four copyright notes stuck in the middle). He also regularized a couple of other details that have since become standard: the first word, *on,* where earlier versions began simply "The first day of Christmas," etc., and "calling" birds instead of the various types of blackbird. Unlike the "rings," however, in these instances it seems possible that was just noting down what people usually sang, rather than adding something of his own.

Much could be written about the infinite variety of musical structure within the narrow confines of the little tunes in this book. This one has a curious cumulative shape, where gifts two to four at first get the same melodic hook, but only until the presentation of gift five, after which they each get a new tune of their own and gifts six and upward get the original melodic fragment. It's an odd way to put together a melody, but very satisfying.

In most versions the gifts are handed over from one to twelve, in some the other way round, occasionally both, forward then backward. Almost all the tunes put the opening and closing refrain in 4/4 and switch to some kind of triple time for the recitation of the gifts, adding a rushing, helter-skelter excitement to the playground memory test.

Some didn't get it. A humorless public-school type of 1869 sniffed at "its peculiarity and the utter absurdity of the words," which of course completely misses the point. Nonsense songs are supposed to be nonsense. Recent wits have had fun pretending to take it literally. John Julius Norwich has composed a set of letters from the recipient to the true love, beginning with delighted surprise and ending with the donor being arrested for stalking. The notional value of the total basket of gifts is used as a light-hearted measure of seasonal prices ($114,651.18 in 2013, apparently, up a worrying 7.7 percent on the year before, assuming minimum wage for the milkmaids, union rates for drummers and pipers, and quotes from reputable aviaries, jewelers and garden centers).

And so we reach the twelfth day. This is the Christmas of revels, of parties, and gifts. And somewhere under the happy surface of this little song lurks the ancient spirit of Twelfth Night.

On the first day of Christ-mas my true love sent to me a par- tridge in a pear tree. On the se-cond day of Christ-mas my true love sent to me two tur-tle doves, and a par tridge in a pear tree. On the third day of Christ-mas my true love sent to me three French hens, two tur tle doves, and a par tridge in a pear tree. On the fourth day of Christ-mas my true love sent to me four cal-ling birds, three French hens, two tur-tle doves, and a par-tridge in a pear tree. On the fifth day of Christ-mas my

January 6: Epiphany

"We Three Kings"

several of the best-loved carols are American in origin. The United States has its own distinctive traditions about how and where to do carols. The Christmas pageant is the equivalent of what the British call a nativity play. Both are directly descended from, and closely related to, the medieval liturgical drama and mystery play.

Its grown-up cousin, the Christmas parade, is a sort of ancient Roman victory march in Santa hats, a kind of Christmas ticker-tape parade, all sequins, songs, and civic pride, with a strong dash of commercialism thrown in. Hollywood hovers like a presiding angel. "We Three Kings" owes something to this semi-theatrical tradition.

John Henry Hopkins Jr. was a clergyman. He worked initially in journalism and the law before studying for ordination at the General Theological Seminary in New York City, graduating in 1850. Five years later he took up the post of music teacher at his old college, combining it with his ministry as rector of Christ Episcopal Church in nearby Williamsport, Pennsylvania. "We Three Kings" was written for a pageant at the seminary in 1857, and published with a number of his other Christmas pieces in *Carols, Hymns and Songs* in 1863.

Like its close cousin "Away in a Manger," "We Three Kings" is a performance piece. An element of staging, actual or implied, is built into the structure. The first and last verses, and the intervening refrains, are in harmony, a universal hymn of praise. Verses two, three, and four are each given to one of the "kings," presenting his gift and commenting on its symbolic significance. These verses can be sung by three soloists, and Hopkins tells us with all the pragmatism of the music teacher: "Men's voices are best for the parts of the Three Kings, but the music is set in the G clef for the accommodation of children." Performers can move around the church or hall, stopping for each verse and journeying on toward the crib during the refrains in a version of the medieval *stations* (the word is related to *stanza*). This is exactly like the very earliest liturgical dramas such as the Easter *"Quem quaeritis"* ("Whom seek ye?"), where individual members of the choir would take the roles of the angel and the three Marys and "act out" the gospel stories in music, hiding behind an altar or pillar and popping out when the stone is rolled away.

Hopkins's tune is in the "Aeolian mode," an appropriately Eastern-sounding musical scale, much remarked upon and occasionally mistaken for a genuine folk song. His words are powerful and direct, at their best when repetition and simplicity of language evoke the swinging, purposeful march toward Bethlehem ("Star of wonder, star of light, star with royal beauty bright").

It's an effective and unusual conception. It's also one of a tiny number of our carols where we know for certain that words and music are by the same person, who he was, and what he wrote. Naturally, this hasn't stopped editors and compilers fiddling around with it.

Why is this still acceptable for hymns, when the whole thrust of modern editorial and scholarly good practice is to try to get as close as possible to an "authentic" version of what author or composer intended? Hopkins didn't like it any more than John Wesley did a century earlier. It brought out the lawyer in him: "Compilers of other Collections are at liberty to transfer any of the pieces in this little volume, provided they leave what they take unaltered. If any change be made in either words or music without my permission, I shall prosecute the offender to the extent of the law." It didn't work, of course.

The hymns in Hopkins's "little volume" cover a range of Christmas themes. By writing about the characters he called the "Three Kings of Orient" he was entering the much-stirred waters of debate about whether they were kings, and whether there were three of them.

It doesn't matter. Scripture doesn't say they were, but it doesn't say they weren't. "Kings" is a convenient shorthand for educated aristocrats.

Anyway, nineteenth-century Americans were supposed to be unbothered about the niceties of noble rank and titles (notwithstanding the observations of Dickens and Henry James). As for their number, the other kings might just be off in the wings, unpacking the odors of Edom or checking the gold of obedience for dents.

Hopkins had hit on something. This carol stood out. It made it into many published collections, not all of them heeding his lawyerly instructions about leaving the text unaltered.

Henry Ramsden Bramley and John Stainer brought it to England in their *Christmas Carols New and Old* of 1878. Between the great carol collectors of the mid-nineteenth century (Sandys, Husk, Sylvester, etc.) and the folklorists of the turn of the twentieth (Sharp, Baring-Gould, Vaughan Williams), the compilers of the first carol books for choirs are among the heroes of this story. Their job was to provide something people would want to use. The repertoire we know today was to a large extent assembled and codified by them. Bramley and Stainer were among the first, most serious, most musical, and best of the arranger editors. These two kings of caroling are the great-granddaddies of the "University" carol books, the "Cowley" carol book, and every similar collection since.

The three kings and their carol have had their fair share of parody, perhaps because, like the shepherds with their socks, they are not part of the Holy Family or celestial choir, which makes them fair game. In the story, they represent us, so we can share a joke with them.

Very young children can still quite easily be reduced to helpless giggles by songs of the variety:

We Three Kings of Orient are
One in a taxi, one in a car,
One on a scooter, tooting his hooter,
Eating a chocolate bar.

A Christmas sermon might begin with an account of a nativity play, like this one:

The first king steps forward and says, "Gold."

"Myrrh," proclaims the second.

The third strides to the front of the stage and announces, "Frank sent this."

The American pageant and parade created a distinctive subset of Christmas songs. Theatrical, colorful and inclusive, they lead directly into the world of "Jingle Bells" and the Irving Berlin of "White Christmas" and "Easter Parade." These are secular, seasonal party songs. This is what carols were for before they involved the sacred.

Hopkins gets his kings to reflect for us on the whole of the message of Christ's coming, from their summoning by the star to the symbolic presence of the "stone-cold tomb." He picks up some very ancient themes. The "Carol of the Star" is one of our oldest written carols. Folk carols like the "Cherry Tree" and the "Dancing Day" embrace the whole Christian worldview from Christmas to Easter, as Hopkins does.

The "star of wonder" has been guiding poets and musicians to its perfect light for a long time.

"We Three Kings"

CASPAR:

Born a King on Bethlehem plain,
Gold I bring to crown Him again,
King forever,
Ceasing never
Over us all to reign.
Refrain

BALTHAZAR:

Myrrh is mine; it's bitter perfume;
Breathes a life of gathering gloom:—
Sorrowing, sighing,
Bleeding, dying,
Sealed in the stone-cold tomb.
Refrain

MELCHIOR:

Frankincense to offer have I;
Incense owns a Deity nigh:
Prayer and praising
All men raising,
Worship Him God on high.
Refrain

ALL:

Glorious now behold Him arise,
King and God and sacrifice.
Heav'n sings Hallelujah;
Hallelujah the earth replies.
Refrain

"What Child Is This?"

et the sky rain potatoes! Let it thunder to the tune of "Green Sleeves"!

Shakespeare mentions "Greensleeves" twice in *The Merry Wives of Windsor*. The other mention has nothing to do with potatoes:

> I shall think the worse of fat men, as long as I have an eye to make difference of men's liking. And yet he would not swear; praised women's modesty; and gave such orderly and well-behaved reproof to all uncomeliness, that I would have sworn his disposition would have gone to the truth of his words: but they do no more adhere and keep pace together, than the Hundredth Psalm to the tune of Green Sleeves.[1]

There are two points of interest here. The first is that "Greensleeves" was obviously well enough known by around 1597, when Shakespeare wrote this play (apparently at the personal request of the Queen, who wanted more of her favorite fat man, Falstaff), for him to name-check it and expect his audience to get the reference. The second is that even by that date people were singing this tune with all sorts of words. Mistress Ford is referring to the practice of using folk songs, or any other kind of well-known tune, to sing metrical versions of the psalms (that is, rhyming and in a regular meter). The practice was widespread from the mid-sixteenth century, and it's no surprise to find "Greensleeves" being recruited for this purpose.

This is the tradition to which William Chatterton Dix and John

Stainer were contributing when they made the tune of Green Sleeves adhere and keep place together with the poem "What Child Is This?" in the late nineteenth century.

Before it got to that point, this lovely little tune had plenty of other words sung to it. William Chappell made a methodical study of its origins and use in his *Popular Music of the Olden Time* of 1859. Chappell was the father of musical antiquarianism and still one of the best. He tells us that "Greensleeves" was first recorded in 1580, already popular and therefore certainly much older. Although he thinks it "must be a tune of Henry's reign," he certainly didn't set running the old hare that "Henry" wrote it. He didn't.

Thereafter, the tune was regularly pressed into service to make a political or religious point, often by both sides of an argument at the same time. There are songs for and against Puritans, Catholics, Oliver Cromwell, and the Jacobites. There is even a splendidly scurrilous song about attempts to cover up the fact that the pope had become a father.

On one occasion it had words sung to it to accompany an execution:

You traitors all that do devise
To hurt our Queen in treacherous wise,
And in your hearts do still surmise
Which way to hurt our England;
Consider what the end will be
Of traitors all in their degree:
Hanging is still their destiny
That trouble the peace of England.

Chappell notes that "the conspirators were treated with very little consideration by the ballad monger in having their exit chaunted to a merry tune, instead of the usual lamentation," which may perhaps have been the least of their worries at the time.

Like all good folk songs, "Greensleeves" could simultaneously lend itself to this sort of street-level stuff and to the proprieties of divine worship without batting an eyelid. As early as 1580, Chappell finds

"Greene Sleves moralised to the Scripture, declaring the manifold ben-
efites and blessings of God bestowed on sinful man,"[2] exactly the sort
of thing Mistress Ford, and Stainer and Dix, had in mind.

The carol tradition appeared early in the encyclopedia of texts associated with this flexible and beautiful tune. One song, for harvest, says,
"a pie sat on a pear-tree top," a curious echo of both the apple-wassail
carols and "The Twelve Days of Christmas."

"A Carol for New Year's Day, to the tune of Green Sleeves" was
printed in a ballad sheet in 1642. It is perhaps worth quoting in full:

The old year now away is fled,
The new year it is entered;
Then let us now our sins down tread,
And joyfully all appear.
Let's merry be this holiday,
And let us run with sport and play,
Hang sorrow, let's cast care away—
God send you a happy new year.

And now with new year's gifts each friend
Unto each other they do send;
God grant we may our lives amend,
And that the truth may appear.
Now like the snake cast off your skin
Of evil thoughts and wicked sin
And to amend this new year begin—
God send us a merry new year.

And now let all the company
In friendly manner all agree,
For we are here welcome all may see
Unto this jolly good cheer.
I thank my master and my dame,
The which are founders of the same,

To eat to drink now is no shame—
God send us a merry new year.

Come lads and lasses every one,
Jack, Tom, Dick, Bess, Mary, and Joan,
Let's cut the meat unto the bone,
For welcome you need not fear.
And here for good liquor we shall not lack,
It will whet my brains and strengthen my back,
This jolly good cheer it must go to wrack—
God send us a merry new year.

Come, give us more liquor when I do call,
I'll drink to each one in this hall,
I hope that so loud I must not bawl,
But unto me lend an ear.
Good fortune to my master send,
And to my dame which is our friend,
God bless us all, and so I end—
And God send us a happy new year.[3]

We are back where we started. This is the carol as celebration and a celebration of the carol, hymning the virtues of the village and its hierarchy, with plenty of folk religion thrown in (like the image of sin as the skin of a snake, a flesh-creeping image worthy of the medieval "doom" painters), and a respectful doff of the cap to the Christian God tacked on the end, almost as an afterthought, as if the squire has just strolled stoutly by, roasted capon-leg in one hand, flagon of ale in the other.

This ballad dates from just before the Puritans launched their all-out assault on this sort of "jolly good cheer." By the time the creators of "What Child Is This?" joined the noble tradition two centuries later, things had calmed down a bit.

William Chatterton Dix was an insurance salesman. His father was a doctor and a big fan of the poet, forger, and the romantic period's favorite suicide, Thomas Chatterton. Dix senior wrote a biography of Chatterton and gave young William a florid combination of his own and his subject's names. This upbringing in a devout, intensely literary but commercially astute family led Chatterton Dix into the twin preoccupations of his life: marine insurance and writing hymns.

He was an excellent hymn writer. This is from another Christmas lyric, "The Manger Throne":

The stars of heaven still shine as at first
They gleamed on this wonderful night;
The bells of the city of God peal out
And the angels' song still rings in the height,
And love still turns where the Godhead burns
Hid in flesh from fleshly sight.

Faith sees no longer the stable floor,
The pavement of sapphire is there
The clear light of heaven streams out to the world
And the angels of God are crowding the air,
And heaven and earth through the spotless birth
Are at peace on this night so fair.

Note the subtle internal rhyme in the middle of line five. This hymn, alas for Dix, got itself hitched to a typically purple tune by Joseph Barnby, and never quite recovered. Some of his other poems were more lucky. "As with Gladness" found itself a nice tune (which its arranger called "Dix," which is rather sweet), and has lived happily with it ever since.

Dix wrote "What Child Is This?" in about 1865. It first appeared to the tune "Greensleeves" in Bramley and Stainer's *Christmas Carols New and Old* in 1871.

There is no suggestion that Dix intended his words for this tune. He may possibly have had another tune in mind. More likely not. His many books of devotional verse have titles like *Altar Songs* and *Hymns of Love and Joy*, which imply singing, but don't specify a tune. Like the compiler of Mistress Ford's psalm book, he was content to leave the choice of melody up to his singers. In this case, like Mistress Ford, they reached for their old favorite "Greensleeves." The words don't fit terribly well. But then, the tune has some fluid and unexpected little twists of shape and rhythm that have defeated other wordsmiths, balladeers, and professional hymnologists alike. It's that very unexpectedness that makes it such a ravishing tune.

It's also what makes it so hard to pin down. Like all real folk songs, there is no "correct" version. Editors and arrangers can't agree whether the sixth degree of the scale is raised or lowered and which pairs of quavers are dotted and which aren't. It's all part of the rich joy of the folk song. The marriage of tune and words was inspired. It was probably Stainer's idea. It wasn't perhaps the most obvious match, but it worked. The wise men are given the privilege of following the star and revealing the message of Christmas to the world, and the quiet rapture of an English folk song is given the privilege of revealing their message to us.

What better place to leave, for now, the story of the English carol.

"What Child Is This"

What child is this, who, laid to rest, on Mary's lap is sleep-ing, Whom an-gels greet with an-thems sweet, while shep-herds watch are keep-ing? This, this is Christ the King, whom shep-herds praise and an - gels sing: Haste, haste to bring him praise, Je - sus the son of Ma - ry.

How comes He in such mean estate,
Where ox and ass are feeding?
Yet have no fear, God's love is here,
His love all loves exceeding.
Raise, raise your song on high,
As Mary sings a lullaby.
See, see, where Christ is born,
Jesus the Son of Mary.

Earth, give Him incense, gold and myrrh,
Come, tribes and people, own Him;
The King of kings salvation brings,
So in your hearts enthrone Him.
Nails, spear shall pierce Him through,
Such pain he bore for me and you.
Praise, praise, the Son of Man,
Jesus the Son of Mary.

"Jingle Bells"

ho was the most badly behaved carol composer of all?

James Lord Pierpont would make anybody's short list.

He was born in 1822, the son of a Unitarian minister from Boston. At the age of ten he was sent to a boarding school in New Hampshire and four years later ran away to sea onboard a whaling ship called the *Shark*, apparently getting as far as California, a pretty epic voyage for the time. Young James had clearly found his sea legs. He enrolled in the US Navy and served until he was twenty-one, when he returned east. He married and moved with his wife and two young children to Medford, in his home state of Massachusetts. In 1849 his father accepted a position in the same town, and James, not yet ready for the shackles of domesticity, took the opportunity to leave his wife and children with his father and head out west once more, setting up a business in San Francisco on the back of the Gold Rush and the elusive fortunes greedily dreamed of by the Forty-Niners. Like so many of the dreamers, he lost everything in one of the many fires that tore through the early years of that fabulous city.

James's brother, John Pierpont, followed their father into the ministry, and got a job in Savannah, Georgia. In 1856, following the death of his wife from tuberculosis, James joined his brother down south, becoming organist of his church and supplementing his living by teaching, as musicians have done since the first syllable of recorded time. Once again his three young children, now motherless, remained with their grandfather in Medford.

He also began writing songs.

The art of successful songwriting hasn't changed much over the centuries: catchy tune; words that sum up a sentiment or situation memorably and neatly. This is from Pierpont's rather self-pityingly autobiographical song "The Returned Californian," published in 1852:

> Oh, I'm going far away from my Creditors just now,
> I ain't the tin to pay 'em and they're kicking up a row;

Another verse contains a neat play on the homophones *dammed* and *damned*:

> So I went up to the mines and I helped to turn a stream,
> And got trusted on the strength of that delusive golden dream;
> But when we got to digging we found twas all a sham,
> And we who dam'd the rivers by our creditors were damn'd.

The last verse captures splendidly the roustabout cowboy spirit of men like James L. Pierpont:

> If of these United States I was the President,
> No man that owed another should ever pay a cent;
> And he who dunn'd another should be banished far away,
> And attention to the pretty girls is all a man should pay.

His song list gives a pretty good flavor of the type of society he was writing for, with its social mores and its prejudices: "Ring the Bell, Fanny"; "I Mourn for My Old Cottage Home"; minstrel songs like "The Coloured Coquette"; and, into the 1860s, war songs like "Our Battle Flag" and "We Conquer or Die." The dedicatees reflect the style of musical entertainment on offer: Ordway's Aeolian's, Christy's Minstrels, George Kunkle's Nightingale Opera Troupe.

In 1857 James published a song titled "The One Horse Open Sleigh."

If the point of songwriting hasn't changed over the years, the medium certainly has. These songs didn't reach their market as recordings, of course, but in sheet music form. Style has changed too.

Nowadays, if you want to market a Christmas song as widely as possible, publishers will ask for the piano accompaniment to be nice and simple. Not in the 1850s. For his sleigh ride Pierpont wrote a flashy little piano part, cheerfully evoking the tinkling bells in more or less continuous runs and twiddles in the right hand. Dashing through the semiquavers as much as through the snow.

Meanwhile, James's home life, like his eponymous sleigh, continued on its wild career. In 1859 his brother John's church closed because of its anti-slavery teachings, unpopular in the Southern states as war clouds gathered. John returned north, but James, now without a job, remained in Savannah with his second wife, Eliza, daughter of the mayor, whom he had married in 1857, and a second quiverful of young children. (The children of his first marriage were still up north in Massachusetts, and sadly never seemed to have been given reason to believe they all would be received down south, in the cradle of the Civil War.) When the war broke out James joined the Confederate army, despite the abolitionist traditions of his family. His father, John Pierpont Senior, briefly served in the Union army as a chaplain. The Pierponts thus became one of many families to face each other from opposite sides, one of the many incidental tragedies of that terrible, all-engulfing conflict.

A variety of teaching and organist jobs (and a habit of getting involved in scandal) propelled him around Georgia after the war. A census of 1870 lists four children of his second marriage and gives the age of the eldest, Lillie, as sixteen, meaning she was born around 1854, or three years before James and Eliza were married (though the census may be wrong, of course).

The sleighing song, meanwhile, proved only moderately popular. It's a high-spirited romp about paying "attention to the pretty girls," nothing to do with Christmas. A young man takes "Miss Fanny Bright" for a ride, overdoes the showing-off, and ends up face down in a snowdrift. A rival rides by and laughs at him, but the young man is undaunted:

Now the ground is white
Go it while you're young,

Take the girls to night
And sing this sleighing song;

A second edition of 1859 gave it an alternative title: "Jingle Bells, or The One Horse Open Sleigh." Singers began to notice its catchy good humor. Slowly, its popularity spread. This, of course, meant that subsequent publishers and arrangers considered themselves perfectly free to alter and adapt Pierpont's tune as they saw fit. Pierpont's original chorus, in four-part harmony, has more variety of harmony and melody than later versions. His verse has been smoothed out too. The version we know today is, in some respects, a variation of Pierpont's tune rather than the tune itself.

But in this case his editors, though unauthorized, knew what they were doing. They gave the tune that cheeky quality of circling round and round a single note (in the key used here, eight of the first eleven notes are the note A), something they perhaps learned from Rossini (think of the famous fast bit of the "William Tell" overture). In any event, the Pierpont family kept the copyright, though they never succeeded in making much money from it.

The opening of the refrain as Pierpont originally composed it

Pierpont's words survived more or less intact, (even if the later verses are not often sung these days), complete with a small grammatical conundrum. *Jingle* is an imperative verb, not an adjective, so that "Jingle bells" is an instruction, not a kind of bell. It's a nice point, and an interesting example of a verb form that crops up in other Christmas songs, for example, "God Rest You Merry, Gentlemen" and "Christians Awake."

James Lord Pierpont died in Florida in 1893, apparently still on a mission to live in as many of the states as possible. His family continued its rich and varied contribution to American life: one of his children became a "Daughter of the American Revolution," another a leading physician. His nephew was the financier John Pierpont Morgan, founder of the banking house J. P. Morgan (in some of whose later dealings some of the buccaneering cowboy spirit of Uncle James may perhaps be said to have resurfaced). In passing, it is interesting to note that several well-known American Christmas songs have roots in the Unitarian movement, although since "Jingle Bells" has not even the remotest connection with doctrinal content of any kind this is probably not the place to speculate about why that is.

Well over a hundred years after it was written, the global popularity of "Jingle Bells" led to an entertaining little spat about its origins. In the 1980s the mayor of Medford, Massachusetts, claimed that the song was written there. Not so, countered the mayor of Savannah. Both towns put up plaques claiming to be the place of authorship (one of which, appropriately, was damaged by a snow plow and had to be removed). Local historians weighed in. One claimed to have found a newspaper record of the song being sung by children at a church service marking Thanksgiving in Medford as early as the 1840s, which seems unlikely as the song is completely unsuitable for singing in church, especially by children. Team Savannah point out that Pierpont was their man when the song was published, and that the landlady of the inn in Medford who claims she saw him write it must be mistaken, since the building in question had not yet become an inn at the date she cites.

Who's right? In truth, it's a bit of a nonargument. All accounts refer to a letter that young James apparently wrote to his mother from boarding school in New Hampshire when he was eleven or twelve, celebrating the joys of sleighing in the New England snow, though the letter itself has proved elusive. In the tit-for-tat between the rival mayors, there is a strong hint of a couple of local politicians co-opting a local celebrity in order to drum up a bit of publicity for their town. And why not? The song was certainly inspired by Pierpont's early experiences in the north (there's not much snow in Georgia), and published later, when he was working in the south. In any event, an author doesn't necessarily actually "write" something anywhere in particular. He probably carried the idea around in his head for years, maybe decades. Where and when he actually wrote it down doesn't matter.

"Jingle Bells" claimed another record in 1965 when it became the first song to be broadcast from space. US astronauts Wally Schirra and Tom Stafford sent a message back to base about a mysterious object they saw flying through the night sky ahead of them:

> We have an object, looks like a satellite going from north to south, probably in polar orbit. . . . Looks like he might be going to re-enter soon. . . . You just might let me pick up that thing. . . . I see a command module and eight smaller modules in front. The pilot of the command module is wearing a red suit.[1]

Schirra then pulled out a tiny, four-hole harmonica that he had smuggled on board and treated Mission Control to an impromptu rendition of "Jingle Bells," Stafford on sleigh bells.

Perhaps the Canadian astronaut Chris Hadfield had this occasion in mind when he bagged one for the Brits by broadcasting David Bowie's "Space Oddity" from the International Space Station in 2013 (thereby raising the interesting question of whether a worldwide copyright applies off-planet. Apparently it does).

Songs like this set themselves up for parody. "Jingle bells, Batman smells, Robin ran away" has become such a familiar part of this song's hinterland that it found its way back into the genuine Batman canon. It was once actually sung by the Joker himself in an attempt to wind up the unflappable caped crusader. Traditions merge, so that it becomes hard to tell where the fictional, schoolyard parody ends and the real Batman begins.

Of course there will be some who protest that "Jingle Bells" shouldn't be in a carol book at all. After all, it doesn't even pretend to have anything to do with Christmas, never mind the Christian nativity story.

But carols encompass everything. Way back, a carol was a festive song to keep out the winter chill with a bit of uncomplicated good cheer. "Jingle Bells" can certainly claim its place in that tradition.

In some ways, this song brings us full circle. And there aren't many tunes you can play on a four-hole harmonica.

"Jingle Bells"

A day or two ago
I tho't I'd take a ride
And soon Miss Fannie Bright
Was seated by my side,
The horse was lean and lank
Misfortune seem'd his lot
He got into a drifted bank
And we—we got up sot.
Chorus

A day or two ago,
The story I must tell
I went out on the snow
And on my back I fell;
A gent was riding by
In a one horse open sleigh,
He laughed as there I sprawling lie,
But quickly drove away.
Chorus

Now the ground is white,
Go it while you're young,
Take the girls to night
And sing this sleighing song;
Just get a bob tailed bay
Two forty as his speed
Hitch him to an open sleigh
And crack, you'll take the lead.
Chorus

Epilogue

he glory days of the English carol tradition were the dark, ancient times of dances round the fire and festivals of cakes and ale. Congregational singing, beginning in the sixteenth century with the Reformation, led eventually to the carol being allowed inside the church, and to the distinctive sound of the eighteenth-century Christmas, a sort of mixture of folk music and Handel. Nineteenth-century clerics played a crucial role, writing and translating a large chunk of our repertoire, and unearthing and arranging all kinds of Christmas melodies from ages past. Their high church, Anglo-Catholic style was hugely influential, embracing not just traditional carols, many of which might otherwise have remained hidden, but hymns, ancient and modern, and plainsong. They invented the tub-thumper, the pot-boiler, and the descant. They rediscovered modes and draped them with the beauty of holiness and the dominant thirteenth. They did for medieval music what Gilbert Scott did for Gothic architecture and Tennyson did for the legend of King Arthur: Victorianized it, but saved it. It's all a bit "Merrie England." Amis's Lucky Jim would have recognized it. In some ways they were the Henry Higgins of the English choral tradition, scrubbing away all traces of the accent of the street or the field.

They also invented the carol service. Pioneered (in a Cornish shed) by that most muscular of muscular Christians, Bishop E. W. Benson, and his Dean, Eric Milner-White, the carol service has become so much part of our heritage that it's easy to forget just what a novel and relatively recent creature it is. Earlier generations would have been shocked to find these songs, the illegitimate offspring of Western Christianity and a naughty ploughboy, with their muddy knees and earthy language, at the heart of divine worship, in an actual liturgy, a church service, in church. Good King Wenceslas used to look in, not out.

One result of welcoming them inside is that we have rather smoothed over the difference between folk carols and ecclesiastical hymns. But the difference is striking. Look closely, and the lurch from one to the other is like coming into the cool, carved interior of a church from the open fields outside, or, as Routley put it, "like approaching Wolverhampton from the north by train."[1] Hymns are about what happens in the Bible, with a devotional point attached. Somebody wrote them. Carols are about pretty much anything at all, except, usually, what happens in the Bible. Nobody wrote them.

Twentieth-century composers saw the rich expressive potential of the old texts and started making new settings, often incorporating the sound world of modal harmony and folk song, and the "stanza and burden" structure of the folk carol. The "carol anthem" is born. They made arrangements and quasi-symphonic suites of the old tunes in their own musical style, too, sometimes, like those of Vaughan Williams, quite extended. Compositions and arrangements begin to sound rather alike. Poets like William Morris and Christina Rossetti wrote effective new carol texts in a deliberately archaic style. Musicians also learned to mine the poetry of the seventeenth and eighteenth centuries, of Herbert, Godolphin, Wither, Wesley, and Watts, with some gorgeous results. Benjamin Britten, in particular, found a rich vein of inspiration in the early English carol texts included by Sir Arthur Quiller-Couch in the influential *Oxford Book of English Verse* of 1900.

Later twentieth-century composers started to set brand-new poetry in their carols, sometimes specially written, like Bruce Blunt and Peter Warlock composing "Bethlehem Down" as payment to the landlord of a pub for a bar bill they couldn't afford.

The next stroke of genius was "art" carols with the virtues of the best pop and show tunes. Simplicity with something to say is the hardest thing a composer can try to do. Words have an appropriately old-world feel. The best of the melodies have the same innate feel for Sharp's "unconscious art" of the folk singer as the best of Dylan or Lennon and

McCartney. Harmonies might not always pass the Vaughan Williams test for the avoidance of Victorian sentimentality: the whiff of Gounod occasionally wafts from the page like incense swung from a rattling censer by a lacy little altar boy.

But the composed, "art," tradition of carols for trained choirs is not our subject here, though it draws heavily on community and folk carol singing, with sophisticated, subtle, and beautiful results.

Where now? Is the oral tradition over? Our farm boy does not now follow the plough, whistling his local variant of "While Shepherds Watched." His team is not now ploughing in summertime on Bredon. He doesn't chase a mouse down a hole, cheerfully singing "I'll give you one-oh" as he whacks it with a stick. But he does use his mouse to listen to music from all over the world. Vaughan Williams and Cecil Sharp feared that recording, mass media, and the electronic age would kill off local traditions, because everyone would have instant access to the same things. Like all prophets of technological doom, they were partly right. There are fewer variants of "While Shepherds Watched" sung today, but there are still some. Local variation, fascinatingly, is between countries, not villages—between Britain and America, or England and Scotland—and between religious denominations.

And, as well as potentially reducing local variety, recording and the Internet have of course opened up for us the musical resources of the whole world. An English carol service may very well already contain indigenous songs from Poland, the Basque country, the Appalachians, or Spain. Who knows what might be next? Tinselly English Christmas carols are enormously popular in China. Christianity has been well established in India, Japan, and elsewhere for many centuries now. Where are their songs? Where is the version of the nativity with the water buffalo and the wildebeest? Or some beautiful, lilting raga of lullaby to the Christ-child? Somebody, soon, will have huge fun finding the African or Indian or Inuit equivalent of "Riu, riu" or "Patapan" or "I Wonder as I Wander" and arranging their visa to the English choir stall. There is lots more music out there waiting to be welcomed in to the wassail.

And besides, we haven't finished with our own songs yet. We have tapped the researches of Cecil Sharp and others in the south of England pretty thoroughly, but we have hardly started on the work of collectors like Marjorie Kennedy-Fraser in the Western Isles of Scotland. There are treasures there.

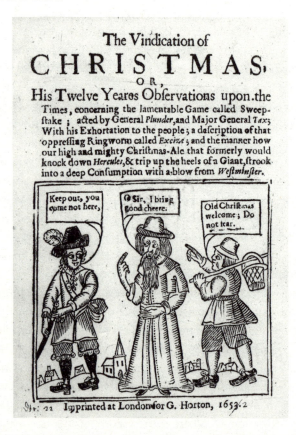

And have the carols we do have stopped evolving? Have we decided whether to sing a passing note at "born the King of a-a-angels" or not? We have not.

There's plenty more evolving left to do. And plenty more singing.

Pass the mince pies.

Happy Christmas.

Notes

Introduction

1. *Sir Gawain and the Green Knight*, tr. J.R.R. Tolkien, ed. C. Tolkien, fp George Allen and Unwin, 1975. (HarperCollins, 2006, Section 3).
2. By William Slatyer, printed by Robert Young 1630, referred to by Joseph Ritson, *Ancient Songs and Ballads from the Time of Henry II to the Revolution*, vol. 2, 1829, p. 15.
3. Joshua Sylvester, *A Garland of Christmas Carols, Ancient and Modern*, 1861, p. xv.
4. Cecil Sharp, *English Folk Carols* (Novello, 1911), preface.
5. Ibid.
6. Sharp, op cit.
7. Rev. Patrick Macdonald, 1784, quoted in *Songs of the Hebrides* by Marjory Kennedy Fraser (Boosey and Co., 1909), "Bibliographical note."
8. British Library Sound Archive, Roy Palmer English Folk Music Collection, shelf-mark 1CDR0010599.
9. *English Hymnal*, OUP, 1906, preface, p. xii.
10. *The Cliftonian*, vol 1, issue 1, December 1867, p. 145.
11. Erik Routley, *The English Carol* (OUP, 1959).
12. British Library Sound Archive, Roy Palmer English Folk Music Collection, shelf-mark 1CDR0007250.
13. Philip Larkin, from the poem "Church Going."

1: "O Come, O Come Emmanuel"

1. Isaiah 11:2, Wisdom 8:1, Deuteronomy 34:9, Luke 2:40, Ephesians 1:17.
2. Mary Berry, from the introduction to her edition of *Veni, Emmanuel* (Paraclete Press, 1983).

2: "O, Christmas Tree"

1. Maria Singleton, *Realized Wishes: A Tale Of Working And Waiting* (London: James Nisbet and Co., 1865), 96.
2. James McElroy, *Andersonville*, ch. 44, "Rebel songs" (1879).
3. Irving Bacheler, *Keeping Up with Lizzie* (1911), ch. 6.

---

4. Joy Winter and Blaine Baggett, *The Great War and the Shaping of the Twentieth Century* (New York: Penguin, 1996), 97.

3: "THE HOLLY AND THE IVY"

1. *Diary of Henry Machyn*, (p. 75), 1554.
2. Sharp, op cit.
3. Ibid.
4. Herrick, "Ceremonies for Candlemas Eve."

4: "I SAW THREE SHIPS"

1. Sir Thomas Browne, "Pseudoxia Epidemica", (1672 edition), Book 7, chapter 7.
2. Routley, op cit, p. 83.
3. William Henry Husk, Songs of the Nativity (London: John Camden Hotten, 1868).
4. Quoted in Louisa May Alcott, *Jack and Jill: A Village Story* (Boston: Little, Brown and Co., 1880), 67.

5: "O LITTLE TOWN OF BETHLEHEM"

1. Ralph Adams Cran, *An Architect's Four Quests,"* by Douglass Shand-Tucci (University of Massachusetts Press, 2005).
2. Mrs. Edward S. Drown in *The Witness*, March 21, 1940.
3. Phillips Brooks, *The Life and Death of Abraham Lincoln: Funeral Oration*, fp 1865, (reprinted, London: Forgotten Books, 2013).
4. Letter, written from Rome on February 19, 1866, to the Sunday-Schools of the Church of the Holy Trinity and Chapel, Philadelphia, in Alexander V. G. Allen, *Life and Letters of Phillips Brooks,* vol. 2, Three Volumes (New York: E. P. Dutton and Company, 1900, 1901), 49.
5. Ralph Vaughan Williams, "A Musical Autobiography," 1950, quoted in Ursula Vaughan Williams *RVW* (1964), 30.

6: "GOOD CHRISTIAN MEN, REJOICE"

1. *The Life of the Blessed Henry Suso*, tr. Father Thomas Knox (London: Burns, Lambert, and Oates, 1865.
2. Wedderburn, (Edinburgh, 1567).

7: "O COME, ALL YE FAITHFUL" ("ADESTE FIDELES")

1. Samuel Pepys, *Diary*, December 24, 1667.
2. Baldwin, D, Programme note, 2013.
3. G. E. P. Arkwright, in *The Musical Antiquary*, Vol. I., April 1910, p. 188–189.
4. "Adeste Fideles, A Study On Its Origin And Development," Dom John Stephan, O.S.B, "Publications" (Buckfast Abbey, Devon, 1947),
5. Stephan, op cit.

8: "While Shepherds Watched"

1. Routley, op cit.
2. Thomas Hardy, "The Choirmaster's Burial," from *Moments of Vision and Miscellaneous Verses*, published 1917.

9: "O Holy Night"

1. Mrs. Kirby, in *Brook Farm Its Members, Scholars, and Visitors, fp 1900 (reprinted.* London: Forgotten Books, 2013).
2. Helen Fessenden, quoting Reginald Fessenden, in *Builder of Tomorrows*, 1940, pp. 153–154.

12: "Hark, the Herald Angels Sing"

1. Benjamin Franklin, *Memoirs of Benjamin Franklin* (New York, 1839), 130.
2. Preface to *A Collection of Hymns for the Use of the People Called Methodists*, fp 1780.
3. William Shakespeare, *Hamlet*, Act 2, scene 2.
4. Letter from Mendelssohn to Mr. Buxton, dated Leipzig, April 30, 1843.
5. "Hark, the Herald Angels Sing!" *The Musical Times*, vol. 38, December 1, 1897, p. 810.
6. Letter from Mendelssohn to Mr. Buxton, dated Leipzig, April 30, 1843.
7. "Hark, the Herald Angels Sing!" *The Musical Times*, vol 38, December 1, 1897, p. 810.

13: "Away in a Manger"

1. See Robert G. McCutchan, *Our Hymnody* (New York: Methodist Book Concern, 1937), 436.

14: "I Wonder As I Wander"

1. Diary of Cecil Sharp, 1916.
2. Quoted on johnjacobniles.com.
3. Ibid.
4. Ibid.
5. Ibid.
6. Ibid.

15: "Good King Wenceslas"

1. Elizabeth Poston, *The Penguin Book of Christmas Carols* (London: Penguin, 1965).
2. E. Duncan, quoted in Dearmer, Percy, et. al., eds., *The Oxford Book of Carols* (Oxford: Oxford University Press, 1928).
3. Dearmer, Percy, et. al., eds., *The Oxford Book of Carols* (Oxford: Oxford University Press, 1928).

16: "Personent hodie"

1. Thomas Morley, *A Plaine and Easie Introduction to Music*, (1597).

17: "Here We Come a-Wassailing"

1. Geoffrey of Monmouth, *Hist. Regium Britanniae* (c. 1140), 113.
2. *Mayor's Accounts of the Borough of Fordwich*, in Canterbury Cathedral Archives, quoted in *Records of Early English Drama. Kent: Diocese of Canterbury*, ed James. M. Gibson, University of Toronto.
3. *Gentleman's Magazine*, 1791, p. 403, quoted in John Brand, *Observations on Popular Antiquities, Chiefly Illustrating the Origins of Our Vulgar Customs* (London, 1841).
4. Fred Hirst, "Decoratin' T' Christmas Tree," http://www.yorkshire-dialect.org/authors/fred_hirst.htm.
5. Routley, op cit.

20: "What Child Is This?"

1. William Shakespeare, *Merry Wives of Windsor*, Act 5, scene 5.
2. William Chappell, *Popular Music of the Olden Time*, vol. 1 (London: Cramer and Co., 1855), 229.
3. Ibid., 228.

21: "Jingle Bells"

1. NASA transcript, December 15, 1965. See also *Schirra's Space*, by Richard Billings and Walter. M. "Wally" Schirra, (US Naval Institute Press, 1988).

Epilogue

1. Routley, op cit.

Bibliography

ibliography, in chronological order of publication. Many of the non-copyright texts listed here are available online.

Primary sources:

Anon. *Piae Cantiones Ecclesiasticae et Scholasticae Veterum Episcoporum*, 1582.

Arbeau, Thoinot. *Orchésographie*, 1589.

Brooks, Phillips. *Christmas Songs and Easter Carols*. New York: E. P. Dutton and Co., 1903.

Tate, Nahum and Nicholas Brady. *Supplement (1700) to the New Version of the Psalms of David*, 1696.

Wesley, John and Charles. *Hymns and Sacred Poems. Fourth Edition*. Bristol: Felix Farley, 1743.

Wynkyn de Worde. *Christmasse Carolles Newely Enprinted*, 1521.

Collections assembled by folklorists and antiquarians, with music and accompanying essays:

Chappell, William. *Popular Music of the Olden Time*. London: Cramer, Beale and Chappell, 1855.

Gilbert, Davies. *Some Ancient Christmas Carols, with the Tunes to Which They Were Formerly Sung in the West of England*. Collected by D. Gilbert. London: J. Nichols and Son, 1822.

Husk, William Henry. *Songs of the Nativity; Being Christmas Carols, Ancient and Modern*, 1868.

Rimbault, Edward F. *A Little Book of Christmas Carols*. London: Cramer, Beale and Co., 1846.

Sandys, William. *Christmas Carols Ancient and Modern*. London, Richard Beckley, 1833.

Sylvester, Joshua. *A Garland of Christmas Carols, Ancient and Modern*. London: John Camden Hotten, 1861.

Wright, Thomas. *Specimens of Old Christmas Carols, Selected from Manuscripts and Printed Books*. The Percy Society, 1841.

Field collections, all with illuminating essays:

Baring-Gould, Sabine. *Songs and Ballads of the West*. London: Methuen and Co., 1890.

Broadwood, Lucy E. and J. A. Fuller Maitland. *English Country Songs*. London: The Leadenhall Press, 1893.

Fraser, Marjorie Kennedy and Kennet MacLeod. *Songs of the Hebrides*. London: Boosey and Co., 1909.

Sharp, Cecil J. *English Folk-Carols*. London: Novello and Co., Ltd., 1911.

Carol-books:

Bramley, Henry Ramsden and John Stainer. *Christmas Carols New and Old*. London: Novello, Ewer and Co., ca 1878.

Dearmer, Percy and Ralph Vaughan Williams (eds.). *The English Hymnal*. London, 1906.

Keyte, Hugh, Andrew Parrott, and Clifford Bartlett (eds). *New Oxford Book of Carols*. 1998.

Neale, John Mason and Thomas Helmore (compilers and arrangers). *Carols for Christmas-Tide*. London, 1853.

Poston, Elizabeth. *The Penguin Book of Christmas Carols*. London, 1965.

Shaw, Martin and Percy Dearmer. *The English Carol Book, First Series*. London: A. R. Mowbray and Co., Ltd., 1913.

Shaw, Martin, Percy Dearmer, and Ralph Vaughan Williams (eds.). *The Oxford Book of Carols*. 1928.

Wood, Charles and George Ratcliffe Woodward (eds). *The Cambridge Carol-Book, Being Fifty-Two Songs for Christmas, Easter, and Other Seasons*. London: Society for Promoting Christian Knowledge, 1924.

Woodward, George Ratcliffe. *The Cowley Carol Book for Christmas, Easter and Ascension-tide*. 1922.

Books, scholarly editions and articles:

Rickert, Edith. *Ancient English Christmas Carols: 1400–1700*. London: Chatto and Windus, 1910.

Hill, Richard S. *Not So Far Away in a Manger, FORTY-ONE SETTINGS OF AN AMERICAN CAROL*. Music Library Association "Notes." December, 1945, Second Series, Vol. III, No. 1.

Stéphan, Dom John, OSB. *The Adeste Fideles: A Study on Its Origin and Development*. Devon: Buckfast Abbey Publications, 1947.

Stevens, John (ed.). *Musica Britannica*, vol. 4. "Mediaeval Carols." Stainer and Bell, 1954.

Routley, Erik. *The English Carol*. Oxford University Press, 1959.

List of Illustrations

p. 52 "In Dulci Jubilo," 1582. Courtesy IMSLP/Petrucci Music Library.

p. 64 The "Air Anglois," as copied by Arkwright, 1910.

p. 65 Pages 91–95 of Wade's *Jacobite* ms (*c*. 1740 or 1744), now lost, as reproduced photographically by Stéphan in 1947.

p. 70 From "The Acts of the Apostles," C. Tye, 1553, parts of pages 52 and 53.

p. 91 Dancers, from *Orchésographie*, 1582. Courtesy IMSLP/Petrucci Music Library.

p. 92 Dance steps, ibid. *Orchésographie*, 1582. Courtesy IMSLP/Petrucci Music Library.

p. 114 Charles Wesley, manuscript of *Hark, how all the welkin rings* classmark MA. 1977/423, copyright of The University of Manchester.

p. 120 Copy of "Luther's Cradle Song" from *The Myrtle*, May 1884.

p. 144 "Piae Cantiones," Courtesy: IMSLP/Petrucci Music Library.

p. 146 "Piae Cantiones," Courtesy: IMSLP/Petrucci Music Library.

p. 148 "Piae Cantiones," Courtesy: IMSLP/Petrucci Music Library.

p. 170 Title page from the first known publication of "The 12 Days of Christmas," *Mirth without Mischief* (1780), ECCO Print edition.

p. 200 "The Vindication of Christmas, or, His Twelve Yeares Observations," 1653 (woodcut and letterpress), English School, (17th century) © Private Collection/Bridgeman Images.

While every effort has been made to contact copyright-holders of illustrations, the author and publishers would be grateful for information about any illustrations where they have been unable to trace them, and would be glad to make amendments in further editions.

Index

 Page numbers in *italics* indicate illustrations. Page numbers in **bold** indicate music set with lyrics for selected carols.

INDEX

K

Karpeles, Maud, 129
Keeping up with Lizzie (Bacheller), 16–17
Kennedy-Fraser, Marjorie, xvi, 42, 200
Keyte, Hugh, 147
King, Martin Luther, Jr., 39
"Kings of Cologne" legend, 33
Kirkpatrick, William J., 123
Knox, Father Thomas: *"Leben Seuses"* (or *"Vita"*) (trans.), 49

L

Labour Party (British), 12, 17
Lacey, T. A., 6, 7
La Mas Ubhal, 158
"Lamb's Wool," 157, 158
Larkin, Philip, xx
La Rose de Péronne (Adam), 77
Lassus, Roland de, 14
Latin
    in fourth antiphon of "seven 'O's,'" 5
    in macaronic texts, xx, 50–51, 145
    in "Noëls," 63
    "Personent hodie," 145, 146
    in "Veni, veni Emmanuel," 6
Laurey, Emily, 77
Laurey, Pierre, 77
"Lauriger Horatius" tune, 15
"Lay a Garland," 53
"Leben Seuses," 49
Leeds, Duke of (Francis Osborne), 57, 60
Lenin, Vladimir, 12
Lennon, John, 129, 198
Libera me, 8
"Light's Abode, Celestial Salem," 100
Lincoln, Abraham, 39, 41, 121
lining-out, 72
Lisbon, Portugal, 8, 9, 59, 60
Little Walsingham, Norfolk, 92
Loewe, Carl, 15
Longfellow, Henry, 16
Lords of Misrule, 158, 166
Lord's Prayer, 71
Louis XIV (king of France), 101
"Love's Redeeming Work Is Done," 111
Ludmila of Bohemia (grandmother of Wenceslas), 136
Luke, Saint, 168
lullabies, 48
Luther, Martin, xix, 48, 50, 54, 120, 121, 124, 146
Lutheran
    Church, 145
    hymnals, 50
    music-making, 51
    psalters, ix
"Luther's Cradle Hymn," 121, 123

Lyra Davidica, 53, 111

M

macaronic texts, x, 50–51, 53, 93, 100, 145, 149
Macdonald, Rev. Patrick, xvi
MacFarland, Dr. John T., 122
Madan, Martin, 109
Madeira, 8
magi (the Three Kings; three wise men), 33, 58, 82
Magnificat, 4
Manchester United football club, 12, 17
"Manger Throne, The," 185
Marbecke, John, 7–8
marching songs, 48
Margaret Street Chapel, Marylebone, London (later All Saints'), 58–59
Marie Antoinette, 97
Mark, Saint, 168
"Marseillaise réligieuse," 80
Mary, Virgin, 28, 31, 32, 33
Mary II of England, xi
Marx, Karl, 83
"Maryland, My Maryland," 15, 16, 17
Mason, Lowell, 124
Mass, the, 96
Matthew, Saint, 168
"Matthew, Mark, Luke and John" (verse), 168
Mayflower, 40, 131
McCartney, Paul, 129, 199
McElroy, John, 16
Medford, MA, 188, 192
medieval liturgical drama, 176, 177
melisma, 93, 100, 139
"Mendelssohn," 106
Mendelssohn, Felix, 106, 111–13, 115
    Elijah, 113
"merry organ," 22, 23
Merry Wives of Windsor, The (Shakespeare), 181
"Messe de Minuit" (Charpentier), 96–97
Messiah (Handel), 110
Methodism, 106
Michael (archangel), 29
Milner-White, Eric, 197
Mirth Without Mischief, (children's song book), 169, *170*
Montgomery, James, 78, 97–99, 100–1
    "An Indian Mother About to Destroy Her Child," 98
Moravians, 111
Morgan, Annie, 130, 131, 132
Morley, Thomas, 29, 90, 145
Morris, William, 39, 198
Motets for the Year (Webbe), 57
"Mueller," 124
Mueller, Carl, 124

213

About the Author

ndrew Gant is a composer, choirmaster, church musician, university teacher, and writer. He has directed many leading choirs including Guards Chapel, Worcester College, Oxford, and Her Majesty's Chapel Royal in London. He lectures in Music at St. Peter's College, Oxford, and lives in Oxford with his wife and their three children.